SUPERMARINE ROLLS-ROYCE S6B

1931 (S1595 and S1596)

First published in December 2018

A catalogue record for this book is available from the British Library.

ISBN 978 1 78521 226 0

Library of Congress control no. 2018953063

Published by Haynes Publishing,
Sparkford, Yeovil,
Somerset BA22 7JJ, UK.
Tel: 01963 440635
Int. tel: +44 1963 440635
Website: www.haynes.com

Haynes North America Inc.,
859 Lawrence Drive, Newbury Park,
California 91320, USA.

Printed in Malaysia.

Senior Commissioning Editor: Jonathan Falconer
Copy editor: Jonathan Falconer
Proof reader: Penny Housden
Indexer: Peter Nicholson
Page design: James Robertson

SUPERMARINE ROLLS-ROYCE S6B

1931 (S1595 and S1596)

Owners' Workshop Manual

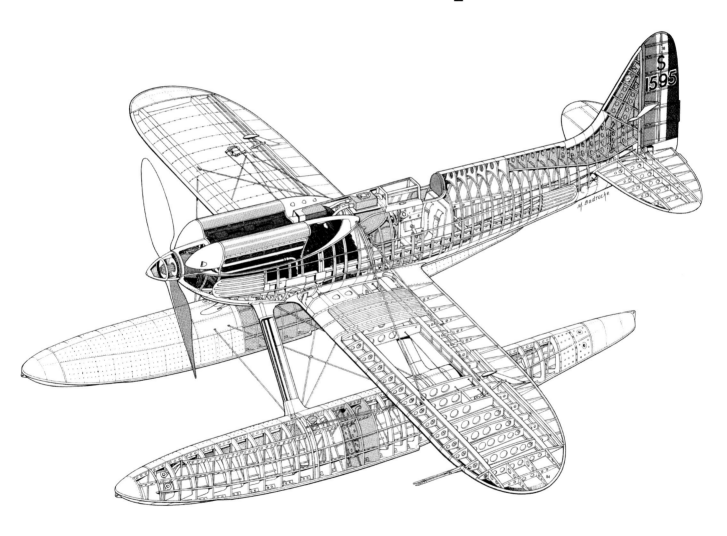

Record-breaking racing seaplane, winner of the Schneider Trophy and forerunner of the legendary Spitfire

Ralph Pegram

Contents

OPPOSITE The Supermarine Rolls-Royce S6 over the Solent.
(All photos are from author's collection except where credited otherwise)

Acknowledgements

The majority of the racing aircraft and engines built to compete for the Schneider Trophy were designed and constructed behind a wall of secrecy and developed under great pressure, tackling problems as they arose within a very limited period of time. The failure rate was high. It is hardly surprising, therefore, that there was little opportunity and even less incentive to document the design process, the details of construction or the results of flight-testing, and hence their story is often piecemeal or brief at best. In Britain, however, the decision to provide public funding for aircraft to participate in the later contests led to a significant body of research work being published as technical reports. Spurred by their success in the closing three contests, some who participated in the programme took the time to place on record a great deal of additional information, either as papers and presentations to clubs and societies or in the form of personal recollections. There are, of course, a few notable gaps and some inconsistencies, but overall the genesis of Supermarine's family of triumphant racers, culminating with the Supermarine Rolls-Royce S6B, can be tracked with confidence.

It is only right to acknowledge those who took the trouble to ensure that the information pertaining to the whole British effort was preserved, especially for the Supermarine aircraft. William Cowley, on the staff of the National Physical Laboratory, was responsible for editing and compiling for publication the diverse work of the multitude of government and industry research technicians engaged on the project from 1926 through to 1931 and ensured that these were comprehensive. Reginald Mitchell, Supermarine's Chief Designer, and his deputy, Frank Holroyd, both presented papers outlining design aspects of the company's racing aircraft; and Augustus Orlebar, commanding officer of the RAF's High Speed Flight in 1929 and 1931, gave several presentations in which he described his experience of flying the racers and also ensured that technical material regarding the flight-testing phase of the S6 series of aircraft was gathered together as an official report. He also took time to rework his personal diary, written while preparing for the contests, as a book. High Speed Flight pilots Harry Schofield, David D'Arcy Greig, Henry Waghorn, George Stainforth, John Boothman and Leonard Snaith all wrote of their experiences flying the racing aircraft in autobiographies or papers. The authors of other articles of note include Frank Rodwell Banks, Pandia Ralli, David Hollis Williams, George Wilkinson and several who wrote anonymously.

I would also like to thank Chris Michell for the many discussions we have had over the years regarding the construction of the Supermarine racers and for permission to include several photographs from his collection.

Ralph Pegram
Hampshire
September 2018

Introduction

La Coupe d'Aviation Maritime Jacques Schneider, commonly known as the Schneider Trophy or Cup, was established in 1912 as a speed competition between marine aircraft, just one among many similar events of the era. Yet as these other contests faded or drew to a close it started, somewhat unexpectedly, to grow in prominence and perceived prestige. Although it was never the intention, the contest slowly fell hostage to the dubious politics of national pride and consequent escalating cost, with endless arguments in Britain and elsewhere as to the true value of participation.

The performance of the first generation of racing flying boats and seaplanes had been considerably lower than that of their land-based counterparts; indeed, many were just land aircraft fitted with crude floats. As the years progressed and funding increased,

the gap closed until a point was reached in 1927 when a Schneider racing seaplane eclipsed the performance of landplanes and took the absolute air speed record for the first time. It would be 12 more years before the seaplane's dominance was lost, and 8 years after the last Schneider Trophy contest had been run.

The Supermarine Rolls-Royce S6B, the sole competitor and winner of the final contest in 1931, was the culmination of a systematic design and development programme into high-speed flight, a partnership between industry and government research establishments,

BELOW The speed of flying boats and seaplanes lagged behind landplanes for many years, but the gap closed when the Macchi M52 took the absolute air speed record in 1927. It was 12 years before landplanes regained their dominance.

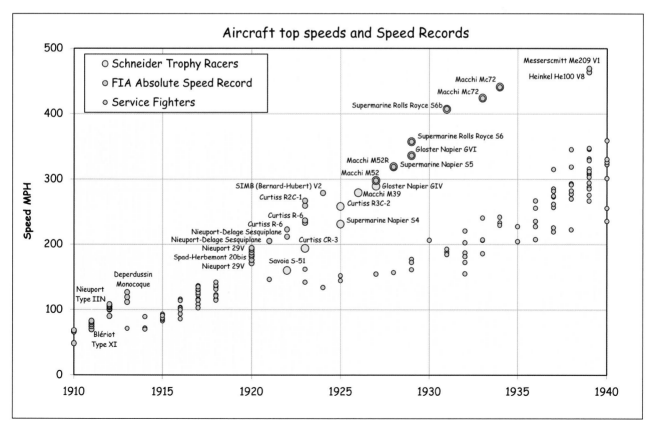

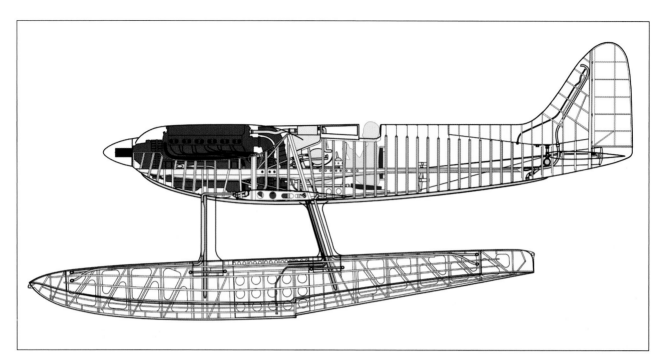

ABOVE The Supermarine Rolls-Royce S6B was described by its designer, Reginald Mitchell, as a flying radiator, with the aircraft packaged tightly around the engine, pilot and fuel tanks.

BELOW S1595, the first S6B, was the Schneider Trophy winner and speed record-holder. Today, it resides in London's Science Museum, its home since 1932.

which spanned five years. It was the last of Supermarine's family of racing seaplanes developed under Chief Designer Reginald Mitchell, of which there were a total of eight: a single S4, three S5s, two S6s and two S6Bs. Between them they racked up one world air speed record for seaplanes and two absolute world air speed records, alongside a number of speed-over-distance and national records. However, this success came at a price – there were also two fatal accidents, three serious

accidents and several close calls; and three of the four S6 family went to the bottom of the Solent. Air speed record-breaking and racing was a high-risk endeavour. The two S6Bs were built in a rush in the spring of 1931 and over a two-month period in the summer they logged just 20 flights between them, totalling less than 7 hours in the air. The longest flight lasted 47 minutes, the duration of the 1931 Schneider Trophy contest.

When the British team secured their third consecutive win to hold the trophy in perpetuity and bring the competition series to a close, few mourned its passing, yet the Supermarine Rolls-Royce S6B with which they achieved this success went on to become something of an icon. It was not just a superb piece of aeronautical engineering in its own right, but it was also an early indication of the growing prowess of Mitchell and his Supermarine design team that was destined to produce the Spitfire – one of the most recognisable and celebrated aircraft of all time – just five years later.

ABOVE The second S6B, S1596, had a short life of just one month. Shortly after establishing a new air speed record, which was not homologated (or officially recognised), it sank after a landing accident and was scrapped.

LEFT The S6B was the epitome of speed for illustrators in the 1930s.

Chapter One

Britain, Supermarine and the Schneider Trophy

Although the support of the government was crucial for Britain's ultimate success in the Schneider Trophy contests, it was the drive and commitment of Sopwith, Gloster, Napier, Rolls-Royce and Supermarine, especially, that proved decisive.

OPPOSITE The Supermarine Sea Lion III was a cleaned-up, clipped-wing modification of the Sea Lion II.

MONTE-CARLO.— Le Meeting des Hydroaéroplanes

The Schneider Trophy contest was held on 12 occasions between 1913 and 1931 and Britain entered aircraft for 8 of these events, with only Italy equalling the effort. They won 5 of the contests including the final 3. In the closing years the effort required to field a competitive aircraft had become hard to justify and increasingly costly, both in monetary terms and in lives, and in many quarters there was a collective sigh of relief that there were to be no more. Half-hearted attempts to revive the contest or to replace it with something of a similar nature received no support. The story of how a simple sporting competition grew to become one of perceived national prestige with Supermarine in the forefront is somewhat convoluted.

On 5 December 1912 at the annual Gordon Bennett banquet hosted by l'Aéro-Club de France, La Coupe d'Aviation Maritime Jacques Schneider was announced as a new annual international speed contest for hydravions, or hydroaeroplanes. The first event was included in the programme of the many sporting competitions to be held at Monaco the following year.

The contest was to be flown over a distance of at least 150 nautical miles (277.8km) and largely over water, with the option for either a linear course or laps around a closed circuit. The competing aircraft had to both take off from and land back on to water and also to carry out some very basic trials of their capabilities on the water, but other than that they could be of any type. Schneider's stated intent was to stimulate the development of practical marine aircraft, yet he chose to establish the contest as a test of speed, pure and simple. Although the rules would have permitted it to have been run as a

JACQUES SCHNEIDER

Jacques Schneider, born in 1879, was the grandson of the co-founder of Schneider-Creusot, a company established in 1833 that had grown to become a highly profitable heavy industry, armament and engineering conglomerate. As a consequence Jacques was a wealthy man with plenty of leisure time. In the early days of the 20th century there were a great many new pastimes for a person in his position, the advent of the internal combustion engine firing the development of cars, motorboats, and, in time, the aeroplane.

In the pre-war years Schneider played with ballooning, motor cars and powerboats before taking up flying after seeing Wilbur Wright demonstrate his Flyer. However, his flying career was short-lived. Just months after learning to fly on a Blériot monoplane and qualifying for his aviator's certificate, he had a bad accident in one of his motor boats and suffered a severe break of his arm, which put paid to any further piloting. He transferred his enthusiasm to the current craze for hydro-glisseurs – shallow-draft punts powered by air propellers – and also returned to ballooning. Although he was unable to fly by himself, he still maintained

LEFT Jacques Schneider was a man with the wealth and time to indulge in sports cars, motorboats, aircraft and balloons.

an interest in aviation and attended many of the flying meetings and flew as a passenger whenever he could.

Why he decided to sponsor a competition for hydroaeroplanes is unclear, and after the initial two contests in Monaco he was not present at any of the subsequent events. He died in 1928.

race, in practice it would always be held as a time trial with the aircraft taking off individually rather than together. As an international competition it would be administered by the sport's governing body, the Fédération Aéronautique Internationale (FAI), and all entries had to be submitted, along with a modest entry fee, via the affiliated national flying club of the pilot's nation, with a maximum of three permitted from each club. The flying club of the winning pilot would become the host for the subsequent contest and any nation that won three out of five consecutive events would hold the trophy in perpetuity and the contest would draw to a close. Schneider commissioned a large silver and bronze trophy portraying water nymphs emerging from a wave to kiss a winged zephyr flying overhead, and for the initial contests he also presented a cash prize to the winner.

LEFT The Schneider Trophy, a silver and bronze sculpture by Ernest Gabard.

1913 – a lacklustre contest

Britain had been just a little slower than France to embrace the opportunities offered by aviation but was developing rapidly. By the close of 1912 there were several established aircraft construction businesses, active flying grounds, and schools for budding aviators around the country. A small yacht charter business had just been established at Woolston, outside Southampton, the seed from which Supermarine would grow.

However, with plenty of local competitions to occupy their attention, Britain's aviators and constructors passed on the opportunity to participate in the 1913 Schneider Trophy, as indeed did all other nations, so that it became an all-French affair. It was a distinctly lacklustre event, marred by mishaps and engine failures, to be won eventually by Maurice Prévost flying a two-seat Deperdussin, which was a last-minute substitute and actually the slowest of all the aircraft that had been entered. It was not an auspicious start.

BELOW Maurice Prévost won the inaugural Schneider Trophy contest flying a last-minute substitute two-seat Deperdussin.

1914 – an unexpected victory

L'Aéro-Club de France scheduled the 1914 contest once again as part of the annual Monaco meeting, for which the premier event was to be the Rallye Ariénne where aircraft converged on Monaco flying over several routes. Many aircraft were entered for the Rallye and several who competed were encouraged to also consider entering for the Schneider contest upon arrival. Entry forms were duly received from at least five national clubs. The Royal Aero Club (RAeC) submitted entries for Britain in the names of Lord Carbery and Tom Sopwith.

Sopwith was a major player among the British aviators of the day and an astute businessman who had established Sopwith Aviation Company in 1912. A small scout aircraft ordered by the Royal Navy, and nicknamed Tabloid, was adapted to become Sopwith's entry for the Schneider contest by the simple substitution of floats in place of the wheeled undercarriage and by the

installation of a more powerful engine. The Tabloid was robust, simple and efficient, and it was entrusted to the capable hands of Howard Pixton, one of Britain's first professional test pilots. The entries from the USA and Germany were withdrawn, and the prime French opposition, expected to be formidable, never materialised due in no small part to insurmountable engine problems. Lord Carbery borrowed a Deperdussin, an aircraft type with which he was unfamiliar, and gave up early on. Pixton in the Tabloid easily outperformed the substitute French aircraft and the small FBA flying boat entered in the name of Switzerland. His win meant that the following contest would be organised in Britain by the RAeC, but war intervened and it was not until 1919 that sports flying could resume.

1919 – an opportunity wasted

Sopwith's pre-war win had come as something of a surprise in Britain and received a lot of favourable press coverage.

It was the first by a British aircraft and pilot in an international competition and, with the war over, others in Britain were eager to rise to the challenge of repeating this success over home waters. It may seem surprising that after four years of war the FAI were keen to restart the contest so soon, but as early as February 1919 they had contacted the RAeC to request their plans for the event. At this date it was still several months before the restriction on civil flying in Britain would be lifted, but nevertheless the RAeC scheduled the contest for September and decided that it should take place at Bournemouth on the Channel coast. A base for the competing aircraft was offered by S.E. Saunders Ltd, the boat and aircraft builders at Cowes on the Isle of Wight, some 25 miles to the east of the contest venue.

The end of the war saw wholesale cancellation of military contracts across Europe and no British aircraft manufacturer was spared. A large proportion of the workforce was laid-off while surplus stock and redundant military equipment was dumped cheaply on to the market, killing off almost all sales of new

ABOVE Howard Pixton leans against the wing of the Sopwith Tabloid HS after winning the 1914 contest.

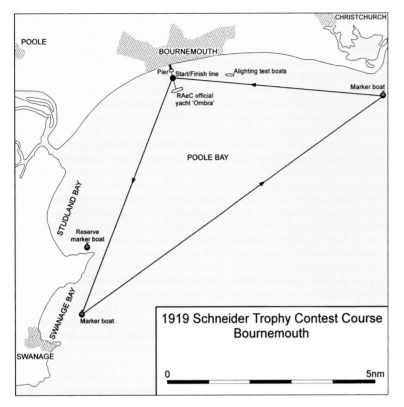

ABOVE Bournemouth Bay, the venue for the third Schneider Trophy contest and the first to be hosted in Britain.

BELOW The British contenders for the 1919 team.

aircraft. Those companies aiming to continue in the aviation business sought means to promote their products.

The four years of war had seen tremendous development of aircraft and, more significantly, the engines that powered them, so air racing looked to be a relatively cheap, high-profile opportunity to advertise a company. Both Italy and France submitted entries while four British manufacturers came forward, so the RAeC would need to hold elimination trials in order to select the three for the British team. Supermarine, a company founded in 1914 as Pemberton-Billing Ltd and rebranded in 1916, were aiming to specialise in flying boats and chose to convert an unfinished flying boat fighter prototype as their racer. Hubert Scott-Paine, managing director, was a shrewd businessman with a passion for speed, hence it was no surprise that he saw the Schneider contest as a perfect opportunity to advertise his company, all but unknown within the aviation industry or among the public. Reginald Mitchell had just been promoted to chief designer and it was probably his first task in the role to ensure that the aircraft, named Sea Lion, was prepared for the race. Fairey took a similar

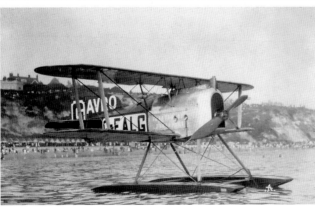

approach and adapted a prototype torpedo bomber by cutting the wingspan dramatically to produce the N10 racing seaplane. Sopwith and Avro, however, both built specialised seaplane racers drawing heavily on their wartime aircraft designs. The Sopwith Schneider followed the company's well-established fighter construction methods and was very similar in size to their 1914 Tabloid racer. Avro's 539 was a small racing aircraft tailored tightly around its engine.

Britain had the good fortune to have two engines capable of delivering around 450hp ready for production, both robust and reliable from the start. These were the Cosmos Jupiter air-cooled radial and the Napier Lion water-cooled broad arrow type. Cosmos was a new company with financial problems yet managed to supply an engine to Sopwith for their Schneider racer. Napier were in a far stronger position with an enviable reputation for excellence and a proven track-record in both automobile and boat speed competitions from the pre-war era, and were eager to showcase their new aircraft engine in the same way. They supplied Lion engines to both Fairey and Supermarine. The Avro 539 had the considerably less powerful, and somewhat

troublesome, Siddeley Puma six-cylinder inline engine installed. The RAeC selected the Fairey and Sopwith aircraft for the team while they arranged a fly-off between Supermarine and Avro, which showed there to be little between them in terms of top speed. The Sea Lion was then chosen due to its superior handling on the water.

A day or so before the contest the French team of three seaplanes set out across the Channel, the SPAD S20bis travelling by boat and the two Nieuport 29s were flown over. They were standard military aircraft adapted for racing. One Nieuport capsized on landing and was hastily repaired by Saunders' workmen, while the other suffered engine failure mid-Channel and had to be abandoned. The Italian Savoia S13 flying boat, a military aircraft with clipped wings, travelled to Britain by rail and sea. The facilities provided by Saunders were first class and the aircraft were well housed prior to the contest. At Bournemouth, however, support was totally lacking.

Bournemouth Bay appeared to be an ideal setting. There was a wide beach and a pier providing ample space for spectators and a ready-made starting line. What the RAeC

BELOW Crowds of spectators made life difficult for the competitors and their aircraft that were drawn up on the beach at Bournemouth.

BELOW Crowds of spectators made life difficult for the competitors and their aircraft that were drawn up on the beach at Bournemouth.

RIGHT Janello and his Savoia S13 flying boat are mobbed by spectators.

WINNER OF AERIAL DERBY   AT BOURNEMOUTH

had completely overlooked was the need to provide facilities for the competing aircraft and their handling crew adjacent to the course. They were left with the stark choice of either pulling up on to the pebble-strewn beach or finding somewhere sheltered to moor offshore, both far from ideal. The SPAD and Sopwith both damaged their fragile floats on the beach while the one remaining Nieuport stayed offshore and started to take on water. Fairey had the foresight to clear and rope off a section of beach to keep the spectators at bay while Savoia found a suitable spot to pull out of the water, but had to endure the attention of the crowd of curious bystanders. Only Supermarine, fortuitous to be a specialist marine aircraft and boat-builder with their works nearby, were well served with their dedicated launch in attendance at their chosen anchorage point.

The contest itself turned into a debacle as a bank of thick sea mist hung around offshore all day. Communication between the RAeC, the course observers and the teams had not been well thought out so there was confusion about what was happening, especially when the start time was delayed. Eventually the contest got under way but both the Fairey and Sopwith returned without completing a lap as they considered the fog to be dangerously thick and were unable to locate the first turn marker. The Sea Lion was holed below the waterline as it took off after landing out on the course to try and establish its location, subsequently sinking when making the obligatory landing later in the lap. Neither French aircraft was in a fit state to start. However, the Savoia, piloted by Guido Janello, took off and appeared to complete the full number of laps and would have won had not the observers at the first turning point reported that they had neither seen nor heard the aircraft. It transpired that Janello had mistaken a second boat as the turning point, the true marker being obscured by fog. The contest was therefore declared null and void, although Italy were awarded the consolation of being named as the hosts for the next contest.

In Britain the whole affair resulted in anger, resentment and a loss of interest in the Schneider Trophy contest, not aided by the RAeC, without adequate consultation, tabling a motion at the next meeting of the FAI that in future all competing aircraft should carry a load of 300kg as ballast. They did so on the assumption that British companies would be more willing to participate if the aircraft were broadly representative of commercial types, but most members of the Society of British Aircraft Constructors (SBAC) disagreed. However, the motion was passed by the FAI and completely changed the complexion of the next contest.

Coppa Schneider 1920.

1920 and 1921 – international indifference

The post-war recession bit hard with strikes breaking out all over Europe and many enterprises declaring bankruptcy. For British companies the prospect of having to travel to Venice for the 1920 contest was not appealing, involving as it did either a laborious rail journey across the disrupted networks in France and Italy or a lengthy, and costly, sea voyage. It was not an attractive prospect and whatever appetite they may have retained for competition was now focussed instead on British sporting events and Air Ministry-sponsored commercial contests. Supermarine, Fairey and Avro were among them. Britain, and indeed other nations, chose to ignore the Schneider contest, which was then held as an all-Italian event – essentially a showcase for Macchi and Savoia flying boats. As was to be expected none of the competitors were racers, they were all standard military types. The winner of the contest that was held in appalling weather was the only aircraft to fly, a Savoia S12 piloted by Luigi Bologna.

By 1921 the level of international interest in the event had not improved despite the inclusion of additional hydroaeroplane competitions at the venue, and once again only Italian aircraft lined up in Venice for the

start. Even the repeal of the ill-advised load-carrying rule had failed to attract entries. The competitors, as in 1920, were all standard flying boats from Macchi and Savoia as the one true racer, the Savoia S21, had been withdrawn at the last moment. The winner was Giovanni de Briganti flying a Macchi M7bis, a type that had been in service since 1918. There had

been little in either this or the previous event to arouse any interest among the public or the aviation industry; indeed there was minimal coverage in the press and the contest seemed destined to expire.

1922 – Italy thwarted

With consecutive victories under their belt Italy was in a commanding position as they required just a single victory from any of the next three contests to win the trophy outright. For 1922 they decided on a change of venue and selected Naples. Mindful that the majority of their aircraft in 1920 and 1921 had been standard production flying boats with modest performance, both Macchi and Savoia prepared dedicated racers to counter any opportunistic challenge from other nations. The Savoia S51 was the second of the company's flying boats designed specifically for racing, while the Macchi M17 had been scheduled to compete in 1920 but failed to meet the load-carrying requirement that year and had not been entered for 1921.

In Britain there were at first no signs that any company was prepared to challenge, even when the date for receiving entries had twice been extended, but then Hubert Scott-Paine approached the RAeC and indicated that Supermarine would be willing to represent Britain if the club would pay the entrance fee. He had bought back three prototype N1B Baby flying boat fighters from the government at the end of the war: the first was retained by the company; the second was modified slightly,

renamed as the Sea King and offered for sale as a sporting aircraft; while the third, which featured a completely different hull and wings, had been adapted as the Sea Lion for the 1919 contest, where it had been wrecked. The Sea King attracted no sales so was reconfigured as an amphibian in 1921 and renamed Sea King II, but it had remained unsold and could be modified quickly as a racer. Scott-Paine had discussed this possibility with Harry Vane, his counterpart at Napier, who agreed to supply a Lion engine at no cost. Similar deals were struck for supplies of oil and fuel, and with a shipping company to provide free transport to Naples. It appeared that they would be able to compete at almost negligible cost and that the aircraft, renamed Sea Lion II, would be substantially faster than any of the types fielded by the Italians in 1921. It was a shoestring operation, but in with a chance.

The Sea Lion II did indeed appear competitive against two of the Italian team's aircraft, although their sleek new Savoia S51 flying boat looked to be a serious rival. Unfortunately the top-heavy sesquiplane capsized during the preliminary trials, but the British team raised no objection when it was recovered, dried out, and hurriedly prepared for the main speed contest. Unsurprisingly it was

RECORD MONDIALE DI VELOCITÀ PER IDROVOLANTI
Km./ora 280, 155 .. .. Sesto Calende, 28 Dicembre 1922

ABOVE Biard rounds the turn marker balloon in the Bay of Naples on his way to win the trophy.

not in good shape and proved unable to match the speed of the Sea Lion II so Supermarine's test pilot, Henry Biard, was able to secure an easy win for Britain and also set new speed-over-distance records.

1923 – the stakes are raised

As the 1923 contest was to be held in Britain once again, the RAeC expected there to be an enthusiastic response from British industry, but it was not to be. Many companies were still financially weak and the

cost of producing a viable racer was looking increasingly hard to justify. The government offered to purchase any aircraft that won the contest for £3,000, but this was little incentive to take on the risk, especially when it became known that France would enter a team of three, part-sponsored with government money, and the USA would also send a full team financed and run by the US Navy. The US Army and Navy had been carrying out a programme of high-speed aircraft development in partnership with Curtiss and Wright since 1920, and both had entered aircraft in the Pulitzer races and other competitions.

RIGHT The Royal Aero Club (RAeC) chose to hold the 1923 contest in the Solent adjacent to Sam Saunders' works where the competitors would be hangared, mindful not to repeat the mistakes of 1919.

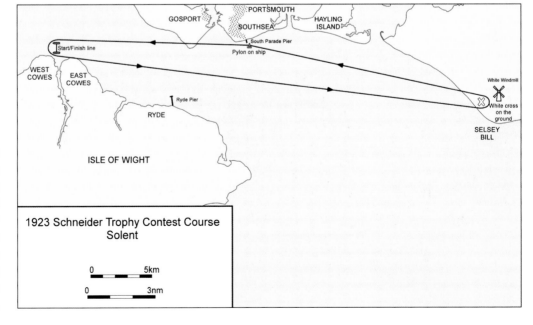

1923 Schneider Trophy Contest Course Solent

As no British company had yet come forward, the date for entries was put back in the hope that someone in Britain could be convinced to compete and defend the trophy. There were rumours that the Gloucestershire Aircraft Company (GAC), who had constructed land aircraft for racing and held the British air speed record, were considering the possibility, but that faded, and it was just before the contest that formal entries were received by the RAeC. There were three: Hawker Engineering, Blackburn and Supermarine; all, it would transpire, to be cobbled together at minimal cost. Sopwith Aircraft had been liquidated in 1920 after receiving a tax bill for excess profits during the war and Tom Sopwith had established a new company, Hawker Engineering. They bought the 1919 Sopwith Schneider from the liquidators, converted it to a landplane, renamed it as the Rainbow and entered for the 1923 King's Cup race. Plans to reinstall the floats for the Schneider contest had to be abandoned when it was wrecked in a crash. Blackburn took an unused 1918 single-seat flying boat hull from storage and used this as the basis for the Pellet, a Lion-powered racer in the style of Supermarine's Sea Lion. Supermarine simply took their winning aircraft from 1922, cropped the wings and applied some very basic, cheap and probably minimally effective aerodynamic improvements to become the Sea Lion III. Britain may have avoided the embarrassment of holding

the contest without a team to defend the trophy, but it was a half-hearted, eleventh-hour effort and known to be weak.

The RAeC reviewed venues for the contest and selected the Solent, the water between the English mainland and the Isle of Wight, where Saunders made their works available once again. Both France and the USA arrived with a contingent of primary and back-up racers which, through a variety of mishaps, was slowly whittled down. France lost one of their Latham L1 twin-engine flying boats when it was blown ashore and badly damaged, and the second failed to make it to the starting line when one of the engines refused to start. The CAM 36bis flying boat collided with a yacht while taxiing to the start line and the CAM 38 damaged its elevator on take-off and could barely complete a single lap. The USA was little better off as their second-string racer, a Wright NW-2 seaplane, was wrecked when the engine disintegrated on a high-speed test flight. The Navy-Curtiss TR-3A trainer was then brought forward as a substitute, but a backfire sheared the drive from the starter and it had to be withdrawn. Britain, however, did no better as the Blackburn Pellet was wrecked when severe porpoising caused it to capsize during the preliminary trials.

The contest thus came down to Supermarine's Sea Lion III racing against two Curtiss CR-3s, which ominously had sailed

BELOW The demise of the Blackburn Pellet, a victim of severe porpoising on take-off.

RIGHT The shape of
things to come: the
US Navy team launch
David Rittenhouse's
contest-winning
Curtiss CR-3.

through all the preliminaries with panache. Vague hopes that they might have faltered in the swell came to nought. These aircraft were seaplane modifications of the Curtiss CR-2 landplane racers powered by Curtiss D-12A engines that had proven themselves in US races the previous year. They were now fitted with the new Curtiss-Reed metal propeller and clearly the fastest aircraft entered for the contest. There was nothing Supermarine could do other than pray that they would succumb to mechanical failure but it was not to be – the USA won the trophy by a wide margin, the aircraft of Lieutenant (Lt) David Rittenhouse being 20mph faster than the Sea Lion III.

1924 – US sportsmanship

The National Aeronautics Association (NAA) scheduled the next contest for the end of October at Bay Shore Park, near Baltimore. The clear supremacy of the US team backed by Navy money and facilities made it abundantly clear that it would be impossible for individual companies to mount a serious challenge without themselves receiving substantial government support. In France the message was received loud and clear and they lost interest in raising a challenge for many years. Italy held a design competition but was hampered by the lack of suitable high-power

engines. Nevertheless construction commenced on a few prototypes, but it was soon obvious that none could be completed in time and their entry was withdrawn in mid-year. In Britain, too, funding remained a serious issue but the Air Ministry did agree to part-fund the construction of racers by Supermarine and GAC, the only companies to show interest in entering, from their limited research budget.

Supermarine were just recovering from something of a hiatus as Hubert Scott-Paine, the driving force behind the company, had clashed with his co-director James Bird, accepted an offer for his share of the company and left. This came on top of a period of serious financial hardship that had almost resulted in the closure of part of the works. The situation remained far from stable but Bird believed that there was still merit in participating in racing, and in order to support their commercial business he and Mitchell planned the Sea Urchin racer, once again as a flying boat. The sesquiplane was to be powered by a special 800hp V12 Rolls-Royce Condor engine installed within the wooden hull and driving a pusher propeller behind the upper wing via a vertical drive shaft and right-angle gear boxes. A top speed of around 215mph was envisaged. However, these plans withered as Rolls-Royce ran into problems with the design of the

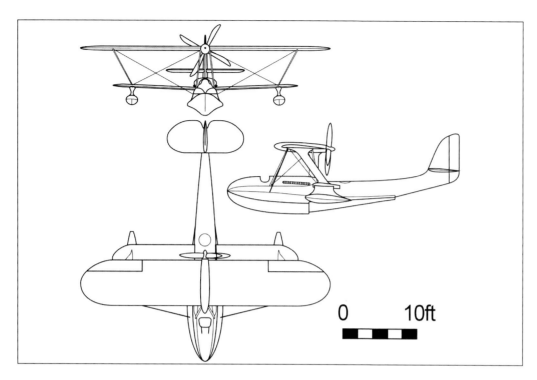

gearboxes and Supermarine had issues with the wing layout and provision for engine cooling.

GAC designed a seaplane with a wooden monocoque fuselage and single-bay biplane wings. The Gloster II was launched at Felixstowe in early September but shortly after it was wrecked on landing when the float chassis collapsed. Immediately after the loss the RAeC informed the NAA that they were not in a position to send a team and withdrew their entry. After a short delay the NAA announced that they had decided against holding the contest without challengers and intended that it should be rescheduled to take place in 1925. This was an extremely sporting gesture and bought the British and Italians much needed time.

During the meeting at Baltimore the two Curtiss CR-3s from the 1923 contest flew over the now-redundant Schneider course in order to set several speed-over-distance records. They also took the opportunity to set a new world speed record for marine aircraft at 188mph. It should be noted that these CR-3s were now three years old, having been constructed as landplanes in 1921 and after continual development were still proving superior to European racers. Even more ominous was the fact that the new Curtiss R2C-2, which would have been the American's prime aircraft for the contest, had not been flown at Baltimore. In landplane form, as the R2C-1, this aircraft had established a new world absolute air speed record of 266.59mph the previous year and, barring accidents or breakdowns, as a seaplane it would no doubt have totally outclassed the Supermarine and GAC racers.

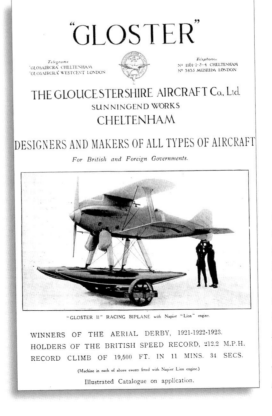

1925 – expectations dashed

The British government's limited financial support was rolled forward to cover construction of aircraft for the rescheduled 1925 contest, and again only GAC and Supermarine were prepared to participate. Notwithstanding the evident superiority of the latest Curtiss racers, GAC chose to refine the Gloster II design to minimise expenditure, and hence the new Gloster III was very similar, with the exception of new Short Brothers-designed metal floats. However, Supermarine and Mitchell started afresh, accepting that a flying boat was unlikely to be competitive against the latest seaplanes and that they would need to design one of their own if they wished to challenge for the trophy. His new racer, to be powered by the Napier Lion, aimed to surpass the well-proven biplane types of Curtiss and GAC by taking the bold decision to be a cantilever monoplane. This type had recently received a lot of attention when the Bernard-Ferbois V2 took the world absolute air speed record for France at the end of 1924. As this was powered by a Hispano-Suiza engine of the same broad-arrow layout as the Lion, it is no surprise that Supermarine's new project shared several of its design features. Mitchell's first concept drawings appeared in late January 1925, the aircraft was constructed over the summer and made its first flight at the very end of August. The S4 certainly looked effective and received positive comments in the press, especially when it established a new world air speed record for marine aircraft of 226.75mph (365.07km/hr) two weeks prior to embarking for the USA.

For reasons unknown the RAeC had entered only two aircraft for the contest but both Gloster IIIs and the S4 were sent out with the British team, the pilots being Henry Biard for the S4 and Hubert Broad and Bert Hinkler for the

Glosters. On arrival at Baltimore they found that the facilities for their aircraft had yet to be completed and they had to wait several days before the crates could be unpacked. In truth, the NAA came close to replicating the mistakes of the RAeC in 1919. The teams were provided with inadequate ageing canvas hangars, erected on muddy tidal flats covered with hastily laid duckboards leading to a rudimentary slipway into the shallow foreshore of the bay, which was being dredged. A violent storm the week prior to the contest brought the hangar down on the S4 causing damage to the fuselage.

The Gloster III and S4 managed one brief flight each prior to the storm, but afterwards the weather and sea conditions remained very poor and prevented any practice flying before the day of the preliminary trials. The Gloster III completed the trials without problems, but the S4 was less fortunate and was wrecked after crashing into the sea. Observers generally agreed that the pilot had executed a very tight turn at high speed and angle of bank before losing control, but opinion was divided as to whether this was the result of wing flutter or a high-speed stall. The second Gloster III was hurriedly assembled as a substitute but while Hinkler was carrying out the trials the float chassis collapsed in the heavy swell, a repeat of the fate of the Gloster II the previous year.

Italy brought two cantilever monoplane Macchi M-33 flying boats powered by standard Curtiss D-12 engines. Although they were clean, well-proportioned aircraft they looked unlikely to pose much of a threat to the British and US racers. The US team, a joint effort between the

BELOW The sad demise of the S4 was the turning point in Britain's attitude towards the Schneider Trophy.

RIGHT The Curtiss R3C-2 was as dominant in 1925 as had been the CR-3 in 1923 and Europe had much to ponder.

Navy and Army as funding was becoming an issue, flew three Curtiss R3C-2 seaplanes that came to Baltimore straight from winning the Pulitzer Trophy race where, as landplanes, they were designated R3C-1. Their Curtiss V-1400 engines were new, evolved from the D-12, and fitted with improved Curtiss-Reed propellers.

In the contest the engine of one of the Macchis refused to start and the other lapped at speeds lower than that of the Curtiss CR-3s in 1923. Broad in the Gloster III was clearly having control problems on the turns but lapped consistently just below 200mph. The Curtiss was in a different class, attaining lap speeds of well over 220mph, but the V-1400 proved to be its Achilles heel with two of the three aircraft failing on the course. However, Lt Jimmy Doolittle's aircraft did not falter, it lapped at over 230mph and won by a large margin, and he then went on to retake the world air speed record for marine aircraft at 245.75mph (395.5km/hr).

1926 – Mussolini fights back

For the British it was now abundantly clear that it was no longer possible to field a competitive team without full government funding, and the annual schedule of contests was also thought to provide inadequate time to design, construct and develop new aircraft. While lobbying of Air Ministry and Treasury officials intensified, the RAeC prepared their case for a biennial schedule.

The response from the Air Ministry was positive and plans were put in place to fund a comprehensive research programme into high-speed flight, but this would be unlikely to result in aircraft in time for the 1926 contest. It set in motion the multi-year project that would lead ultimately to the Supermarine Rolls-Royce S6B in 1931, which will be described in detail later. The RAeC request to the FAI and member clubs for a biennial contest schedule with the next to be held in 1927 was vetoed by the NAA, so on 19 March all parties agreed to issue a press release that stated it was '... inexpedient

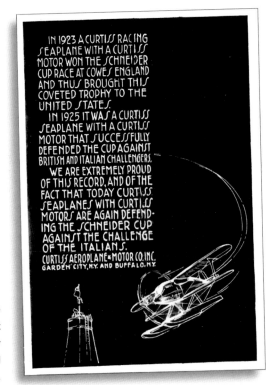

IN 1923 A CURTISS RACING SEAPLANE WITH A CURTISS MOTOR WON THE SCHNEIDER CUP RACE AT COWES ENGLAND AND THUS BROUGHT THIS COVETED TROPHY TO THE UNITED STATES.
IN 1925 IT WAS A CURTISS SEAPLANE WITH A CURTISS MOTOR THAT SUCCESSFULLY DEFENDED THE CUP AGAINST BRITISH AND ITALIAN CHALLENGERS.
WE ARE EXTREMELY PROUD OF THIS RECORD, AND OF THE FACT THAT TODAY CURTISS SEAPLANES WITH CURTISS MOTORS ARE AGAIN DEFENDING THE SCHNEIDER CUP AGAINST THE CHALLENGE OF THE ITALIANS.
CURTISS AEROPLANE•MOTOR CO.INC.
GARDEN CITY,N.Y. AND BUFFALO,N.Y.

RIGHT Curtiss and the US team were at first confident that they could pull off a third and conclusive win.

LEFT Mario Castoldi was the first to field an aerodynamically clean, low-wing, braced monoplane seaplane racer. The Macchi M39 and its Fiat AS2 engine just had the edge over Curtiss's biplanes.

for the Royal Aero Club to make a challenge for the Schneider Cup this year'. They had gambled that the NAA would receive no entries for the contest and would therefore, as in 1924, postpone it to 1927 rather than fly uncontested to win the trophy in perpetuity, with a side bet that the FAI would support Britain's request to make the contest a biennial event. They lost on both counts. The research programme would go ahead, but whether the aircraft resulting from this would ever have the opportunity to fly in a contest was now entirely dependent on the US failing to win in 1926, which appeared unlikely.

However, unknown to anyone in Britain, the Italian dictator Benito Mussolini had decreed that Italy would make a concerted effort to win the 1926 contest in the interests of national prestige and to promote the Italian aircraft industry, for which he had provided all the necessary technical and financial backing. Mario Castoldi, Macchi's chief designer, embarked on the development of the ground-breaking M39 monoplane seaplane racer while Fiat provided the AS2 engine, a V12 heavily influenced by the Curtiss D-12. The pressure was intense but progress was not as rapid as had been hoped and they suffered a fatal crash during early testing. Meanwhile, the US effort had run into serious financial problems. After six years the cooperation between the US Army and Navy had fallen apart and the government was diverting funds for aviation research elsewhere, but the Navy felt that they had just sufficient to refurbish the three Curtiss R3C-2 airframes and to fit each with a different engine type to hedge

their bets. The US Navy base at Norfolk, Virginia, was made available as the site for the contest.

After further crashes, catastrophic engine failures, last-minute substitutes, weather delays and flagging morale the contest was run on 13 November. Yet more engine failures cut short the contest for one aircraft on each team, but the Italians prevailed and the trophy was won by Maggiore De Bernardi for Italy. Britain saw that they had a new adversary to contend with but the M39's average speed of 246mph was not seen as too daunting.

BELOW Curtiss dominance on the wane. The R3C-3 had its Curtiss engine replaced by one from Packard and was very fast. Unfortunately it was lost in a landing accident prior to the contest.

FAR RIGHT An
exuberant Italy
planned for a repeat
performance of their
success on Italian soil.
Venice was to be the
venue.

1927 – Supermarine in the ascendant

At the FAI meeting held prior to the 1926 contest Britain had once again called for a biennial schedule and this time it was agreed to by all parties. However, when Italy won the trophy just a few weeks later they thought it would be to their advantage to hold the next event in 1927 and challenged the decision as counter to the original rules of the contest. This was upheld by the FAI's legal advisers and so the 1927 contest was reinstated. It would take place in Venice that September. This, it would turn out, proved foolhardy. Italy, with just months to go, was gambling that a simple revision to their aircraft and engine would prove sufficient. Similar thinking had led to the defeat of the US team in 1926.

The British research programme was about to bear fruit. A specialised RAF unit, the High Speed Flight (HSF), had been founded at the Marine Aircraft Experimental Establishment (MAEE) in Felixstowe, Suffolk, and were busy familiarising themselves with seaplane operations. GAC had refurbished the Gloster IIIs for use as trainers and for research. The new Supermarine Napier S5, Gloster Napier IV and Short-Bristow Crusader arrived over the summer with sufficient time to iron out most

of the teething troubles, although the Bristol Mercury engine in the Crusader ran very roughly and erratically at high speed.

The Italians evolved the Macchi M39 into the M52, with little change other than revised floats and wings with a slight sweep to improve longitudinal balance. Fiat took the AS2 and upgraded it as the AS3, extracting more power by raising the compression and increasing revs

BELOW The Short-
Bristow Crusader
suffered from
engine problems,
but ultimately it was
crossed cables in the
aileron controls that
led to its demise.

by lightening the pistons, which were fabricated from Magnesium. Unfortunately this resulted in insurmountable problems with heat distortion and lubrication. Their development programme ran down to the wire and they were still struggling right up until the day of the contest.

In the USA a lack of funds prevented the Navy from sponsoring an aircraft for 1927 and it was left to private enterprise to come forward if the NAA were to enter a team. A syndicate fronted by Lt Al Williams, one of the Navy's test pilots and former holder of the world air speed record, raised funds to build a racer and the Navy loaned them an experimental Packard 'X' configuration 1A-2775 engine. The aircraft was designed by Williams and a number of ex-Curtiss staff and built by Kirkham Products Corporation. The unnamed racer, generally

ABOVE The British team in the excellent hangars allocated to them at Venice. From left to right: the Gloster Napier IVB, Fairey Flycatcher trainer and two Supermarine Napier S5s.

LEFT Two Macchi M52s moored out for the preliminary trials. They were let down by their troublesome Fiat AS3 engines.

ABOVE Al Williams
in the cockpit
of the Kirkham
Williams racer. The
X-configuration engine
rarely ran smoothly
and the aircraft
suffered from serious
instability in the air.

RIGHT Sidney Webster
streaks over the finish
line to win the trophy.
Oswald Worsley in the
second S5 was the
only other to complete
the course.

referred to as the Kirkham Williams or Kirkham X, suffered from many problems, among which were a recalcitrant engine, fumes in the cockpit and serious drag and stability issues associated with the floats. Test-flying was hampered by bad weather and other delays so Williams requested that the contest be postponed by one month, and the Italians, who were struggling with their own problems, agreed. However, Britain vetoed the request on the grounds that they were about to embark for Venice and there were no legal reasons to grant the postponement. This was harsh but reflected their dissatisfaction with previous FAI rulings and the growing antipathy within some quarters of the RAF towards the HSF participating in contests.

The contest took place between two S5s and the Gloster IVB for the British team and Italy's three Macchi M52s. For the Italians it proved to be an embarrassing debacle when all of their aircraft succumbed to engine problems, one suffering catastrophic failure even as it crossed the start line. Britain would have taken all three places were it not for a fracture in the propeller shaft of the Gloster IVB that forced it out two laps from the end. The race was won by Flying Officer (Flg Off) Sidney Webster in the Supermarine Napier S5.

1929 – the greatest contest that nearly was

On its return to Britain the HSF was disbanded with immediate effect and it was announced that the government would not fund new aircraft to compete in the 1928 contest. Although it was known that some in the Air Ministry had never fully supported the programme this decision was unexpected and somewhat illogical. Nevertheless Supermarine and GAC both appeared to be at least considering producing new racers, both based heavily on their 1927 aircraft. In January the RAeC recommended negotiations with the FAI, pushing for a biennial schedule and for the next contest to be held in 1929. Again there was unanimous support and this time without legal challenge. This relaxation in the schedule and behind-the-scenes lobbying resulted in a reversal of policy by the government and the research programme restarted.

The three Gloster IVs were returned to GAC to have their top wings raised to improve visibility for the pilot and were then to be employed as trainers and research aircraft. A skeleton HSF was re-formed with Flight Lieutenant (Flt Lt) Sam Kinkead as the sole

LEFT Groundcrew of the RAF High Speed Flight (HSF) act as ballast while the Napier Lion engine in S5 N221 is tested prior to Sam Kinkead's fatal attempt at the world air speed record.

pilot, and a plan was put in place to make an attempt at the world speed record. The small group assembled at Calshot and prepared the third S5, N221, for the attempt in early March.

The
SCHNEIDER TROPHY
Sept. 6th & 7th *1929*
CONTEST

THE ROYAL AERO CLUB
Official
SOUVENIR PROGRAMME

Printed & Published by
GALE & POLDEN LTD. LONDON, ALDERSHOT & PORTSMOUTH

PRICE ONE SHILLING

RIGHT **The RAeC programme for the 1929 contest.**

The weather was cold with occasional flurries of snow but the wind dropped so Kinkead set out in calm and slightly misty conditions to make runs over the record course. The few accounts of what happened next are contradictory, mostly unofficial and many anecdotal, but for whatever reason Kinkead flew the S5 straight into the water and was killed instanty. His place in the HSF was taken by Flt Lt David D'Arcy Greig who made a second attempt at the record in November when he achieved a mean speed that exceed the Italian record, but by a margin insufficient to be accepted as a new world record.

With so much invested in the aircraft and HSF the government decided that they should also take control of the organisation for the 1929 contest and set up a joint committee with the RAeC to coordinate the effort. It was agreed that the contest would take place over the Solent and the RAF flying boat station at Calshot would provide hangars and other facilities for all the teams. The Admiralty would take on the task of policing the waterways and provide ships to be used as turn markers, and larger naval vessels would be present and could be used as venues to entertain visiting foreign dignitaries. When the closing date for entries arrived the RAeC had received deposits for three aircraft each from France and Italy and one from the USA. There was every expectation that the contest was going to be a spectacular show for the public and official visitors alike.

In Britain next to nothing was known about the rival teams, although rumours abounded. They were unaware that all was far from well.

In early 1928 responsibility for aviation in France had been placed in the hands of a new Ministère de l'Air which was keen to make its mark. Racing monoplane seaplanes were ordered from Bernard and Nieuport but progress was very slow, largely because the engine that was to power them, a 12-cylinder broad-arrow from Hispano-Suiza, suffered from endless delays. No aircraft had flown by the summer of 1929 and the team entry had to be withdrawn.

In the USA, Lt Al Williams had raised funding for a new mid-wing monoplane named the Mercury Racer, and the Navy had agreed for it to be designed and constructed at the Naval Aircraft Factory and to be powered by an improved version of their Packard 'X' that he had used in 1927. It was effectively a Navy racer. Construction suffered delays, the aircraft

LEFT French aircraft for the 1929 contest were way behind schedule and the team had to be withdrawn. Here the Bernard racers (top) and Nieuport (bottom) sit in the hangars where they spent most of their time.

RIGHT The Mercury Williams racer roars down the Severn River at Anapolis. Sadly this is as far as it got, becoming airborne briefly for just a few feet.

BELOW The Italian team aircraft at Calshot. In the water the Macchi M67 and M52R; onshore, for display and not destined to fly, the Savoia Marchetti S65 and Fiat C29.

turned out to be seriously overweight and despite frantic efforts it proved impossible for Williams to achieve take-off. Time ran out.

The Italians, and especially Mussolini, had been wounded by the abject failure of their team on home soil in 1927. Their effort was redoubled for 1929, firstly by establishing an equivalent to the HSF, the Reparto Alta Velocita (RAV), and secondly by sponsoring a design competition for new racers and engines; they were not to repeat the all-eggs-in-one-basket approach of 1926 and 1927. Castoldi had

lost faith in Fiat and so his Macchi M67 was to be powered by a new 18-cylinder broad-arrow-type from Isotta Fraschini, but this turned out to be a mistake as the engine was very unreliable. The aircraft also proved difficult to control in the air and led to the death of the RAV's team leader, Captain (Capt) Giuseppe Motta. Fiat did not take the sleight of Macchi turning their back on them lying down and built a racer of their own. The diminutive C29 was powered by a new compact AS5 engine, but this, too, turned out to be a mistake as it was

dangerously unstable both on water and in the air, which resulted in three serious crashes, miraculously without loss of life. Savoia built the innovative S65 twin-engine monoplane seaplane with the tailplane carried on booms and the central nacelle housing the cockpit, and the two Isotta Fraschini engines installed as tractor and pusher. Development was too slow and it was not ready in time. Finally maverick designer Giovanni Pegna designed the Piaggio Pegna Pc7, a monoplane flying boat with hydrovanes and a complex gearbox system that allowed

power to be transferred from a water propeller at the rear to an air propeller in the nose. Needless to say the idea was too radical and the transfer of power, a manual process under the control of the pilot, was never achieved.

By late July the complex planning of the contest was well in hand but the new British aircraft and engines had yet to be delivered. There were strong hints that the French team would not be coming and the news of accidents and problems with the Italian aircraft had reached Britain. It came as a blow

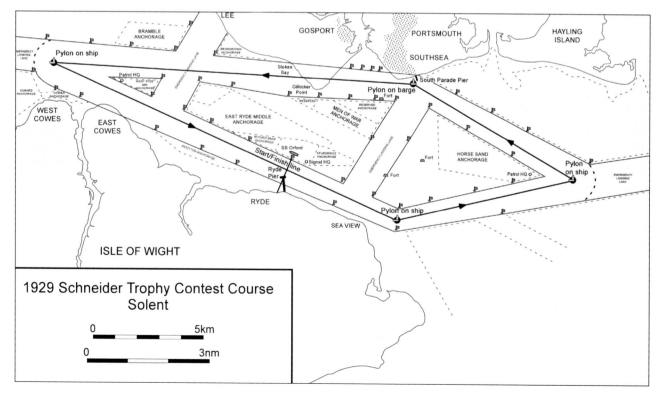

1929 Schneider Trophy Contest Course
Solent

when the French withdrew and the Italians indicated that they would do so too unless the contest could be postponed for a month. With so much complex logistical planning and money invested in the event such a delay was completely impossible, leaving the Italians with the stark choice of withdrawing or fielding an underprepared team. They gallantly chose the latter and arrived with a full team and no less than six aircraft, albeit that one was a trainer and two were not destined to fly.

For the British, too, it had been far from plain sailing. Delivery of both the Supermarine Rolls-Royce S6 and Gloster Napier VI had been delayed and then poor weather had limited the number of test flights. When the

supercharged Lion VIID in the Gloster could not be persuaded to run smoothly at high air speed the aircraft had to be withdrawn and was replaced by the reserve S5. The S6 had required considerable modification, which had only been achieved in a timely manner because the Supermarine works were located just a short distance from Calshot. All issues seemed to have been resolved in time until on the night prior to the contest it was found that one of the Rolls-Royce engine's cylinders in S6, N247, was badly scored and an entire cylinder block had to be replaced (under competition rules) with the engine still in the aircraft.

As the Italians had feared their two under-developed M67s failed to complete the course, each succumbing to engine failure on their first lap. Both S6s went the distance: Flg Off Henry Waghorn won the contest in N247, but Flg Off Dick Atcherley, flying N248, was disqualified for turning inside one of the marker pylons. Greig in the reserve S5 fought a duel for second place with Maresciallo Dal Molin in the Macchi M52R, the world air speed record holder, but proved marginally slower and he had to settle for third place. A few days after the contest S6, N247, piloted by Squadron Leader (Sqn Ldr) Orlebar, set a new world absolute speed record at 357.7mph.

With two wins under their belt and the Italians clearly on the back foot, all looked well for Britain to secure a third and conclusive win. The government-funded partnership between Supermarine, Rolls-Royce, the NPL and the RAE, ably supported by the HSF, had paid dividends. It was a substantial body of work.

ABOVE The 1929 contest was the largest spectator event that Britain had ever held, yet the small high-speed aircraft were difficult to follow in flight and looked a little lost against the backdrop of ships.

LEFT S6, N247, the contest winner, is manoeuvred ashore after a flight, blackened and paint peeling from the exhaust fumes.

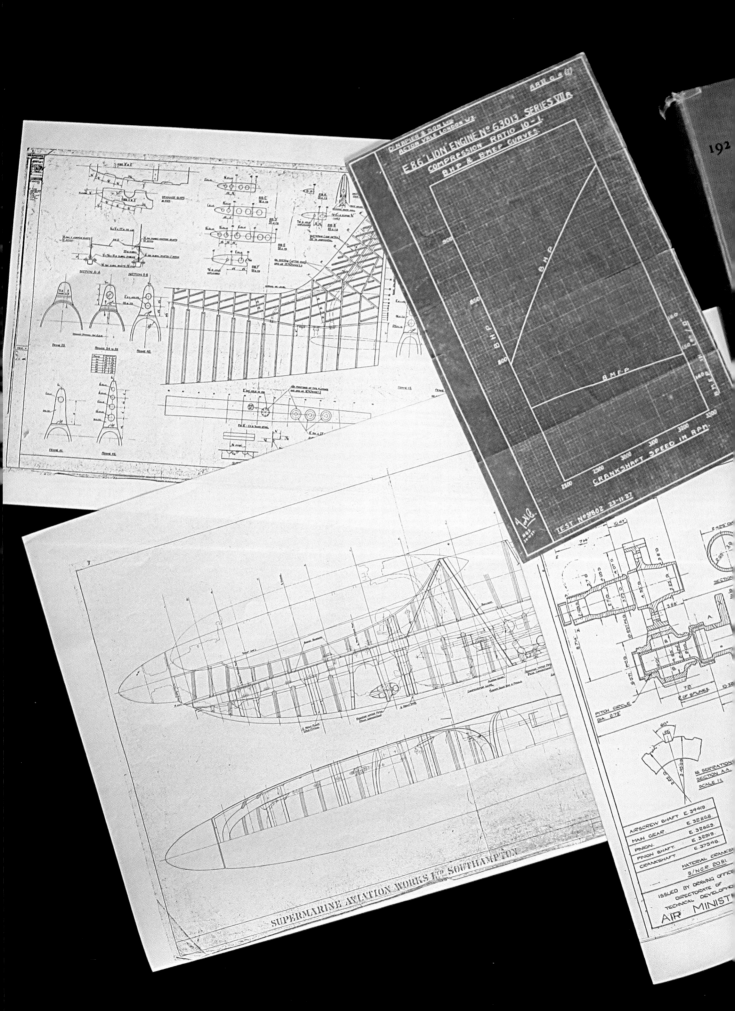

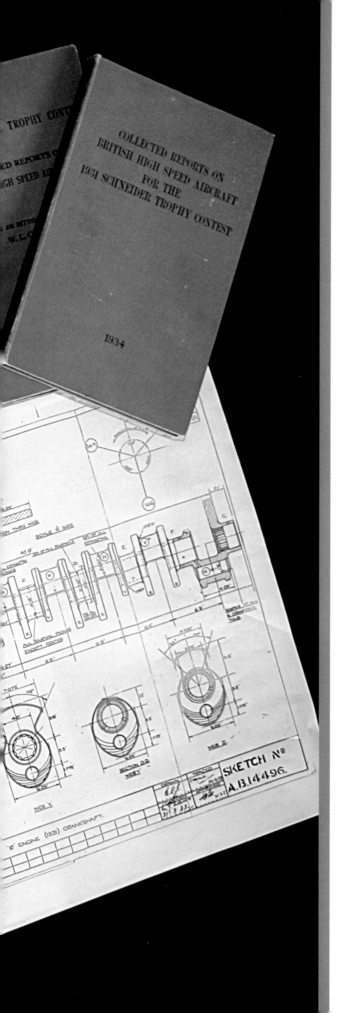

Chapter Two

Supermarine and the high-speed aircraft research programme

Access to government facilities at the National Physical Laboratory, the Royal Aircraft Establishment and the Marine Aircraft Experimental Establishment galvanised research and development of British high-speed aircraft and engines.

OPPOSITE Government-funded research into high-speed flight was comprehensive and diverse. The total cost was never revealed because it was included in their annual R&D budget, but it can be inferred that from 1926 to the end of 1929 in excess of £300,000 had been spent.

The Supermarine Rolls-Royce S6B was the culmination of a five-year state-funded research and development project into high-speed aircraft topped off by a generous private donation. Design and development of Supermarine's family of S5, S6 and S6B racers was a seamless process of continual refinement and modification that allowed Mitchell to improve them in incremental steps, all in close partnership with the engine designers and many technical organisations. At the time they appeared exotic, even futuristic, yet actually employed little new technology. Their success was achieved through careful attention to airflow, drag and stability – no mean achievement for aircraft that flew at twice the speed of contemporary service fighters with engines producing up to four times the power. The groundwork that underpinned development of the S5 was crucial to the eventual success of the S6B.

By 1925 the lead held by the US in racing aircraft, and the air speed records that had shuttled back and forth between them and France, gave cause for concern. Although British service aircraft were not noticeably inferior to their overseas counterparts, there was a nagging perception that the country could soon lag behind in technical development. The Air Council Member for Supply and Research, Air Vice-Marshal Salmond, was well aware of this and had held discussions with representatives of the SBAC before writing a report in November 1925 recommending a government-funded research programme into high-speed flight. Associating this with the construction of aircraft that could compete for the Schneider Trophy appeared logical, although he did not believe that competitive racers could be prepared before 1927. By early 1926 Salmond's proposal had gained government support and meetings were held with Supermarine, GAC and Napier and a consortium of Bristow, a freelance aircraft designer, Short Bros and Bristol. The project was formalised at the end of March. Despite claims written later by both the National Physical Laboratory (NPL) and Mitchell that the intention was to have aircraft ready for the 1926 contest, this was never really plausible.

The project was coordinated by the Aeronautical Research Committee (ARC), the technical advisory body that reported to the Minister of Aviation, and drew upon the expertise of the staff at the NPL and the Royal Aircraft Establishment (RAE) working alongside the technical staff employed by the aircraft and engine constructors. It soon expanded to include medical experts, suppliers of engine components, lubricants and fuels, and a host of others. ARC projects were mostly funded from the public purse and the results of the majority were published as a series of official Reports and Memoranda, and this would be the case for much of the high-speed aircraft programme.

Britain's collective knowledge on aspects of high-speed flight was extremely limited. Little data had been obtained with the Supermarine S4 prior to its loss and GAC's cumulative experience with their Bamel and Gloster racer family provided the only reference for aircraft capable of speeds approaching, or in excess of, 200mph. This applied equally to the engines and propellers necessary to achieve higher speeds. RAF fighters in service were lucky if they could exceed 150mph and were powered by low-revving engines of 400hp, at most, driving wooden propellers. The NPL's largest wind tunnel operated at wind speeds of up to 120ft/sec, while some experimental research had started in 1922 with a small-section tunnel capable of speeds exceeding Mach 1 (the speed of sound). The new research programme would focus on the development of aircraft with an anticipated top speed approaching 300mph, powered by compact engines delivering in excess of 800hp and driving metal propellers with blade tip speeds at or above the speed of sound. A little theoretical and model testing of some elements relating to high air speeds had taken place over the years on an ad hoc basis, but this would be the first time that it would all be pulled together into one coordinated programme. Those carrying out the research had as much to gain in terms of knowledge of their own theories, techniques and equipment, as had the aircraft and engine companies to learn about their designs.

Reginald Mitchell was born and educated in Stoke-on-Trent, Staffordshire, and served his apprenticeship as an engineer with a local manufacturer of light steam locomotives. He completed the apprenticeship and gained his certificate in 1916 at the age of 21. Qualified engineers were required for war work in industry so he resolved to seek employment with an aircraft manufacturer, but it remains something of a mystery how he became aware of and applied for a job with Supermarine as they were a minor company with minimal pre-war profile and hardly known at the time.

Reginald Mitchell (right) with company test pilot and long-term friend Henry Biard.

In the summer of 1916 Mitchell arrived at Supermarine's works in Woolston, a suburb of Southampton, to take up duties as the assistant to the Managing Director, Hubert Scott-Paine. In order to broaden his knowledge of the aircraft business Scott-Paine arranged for him to spend periods of time working within the various departments of the small company, including a short spell in the drawing office, and so his initials can be found on a small number of blueprints produced in the year he joined. In mid-1919 he was working as the Assistant Works Manager when William Hargreaves, the company's Chief Designer, resigned, and Mitchell was promoted to take over his responsibilities. His role was redefined as Chief Engineer and Designer the following year.

In the early 1920s Supermarine's financial position was extremely precarious and Mitchell was in no position to attempt much in the way of new designs. The company eked out a living selling passenger-carrying Channels, a refurbished and slightly modified flying boat type that they had constructed in the war to Admiralty design and bought back in 1919. Hargreaves' N1B Baby in 1918 had also been heavily influenced by the Admiralty's ideas, especially the hull structures devised by their marine architect, Lt Linton Hope. These two aircraft types provided the template for most of Mitchell's early work and so his first designs were little more than simple variations upon the same themes.

It was only when the company had regained a measure of financial security that significant new elements appeared in Mitchell's work when he introduced the twin-engine Swan and Southampton. It was at this point that the S4 appeared, a radical aircraft for Supermarine and unrelated in any way to the preceding flying boats.

Time would show that, paramount among Mitchell's strengths, was his ability as a true team leader. He was a thoughtful man who would listen attentively to the opinions of those in his design team, encourage an open debate among them, willing to give them the opportunity to develop ideas of their own, and with the confidence to incorporate their work into the designs he initiated and approved. Certainly he was critical when criticism was appropriate, short-tempered with work he considered substandard, and at times prone to doubt and slow to make final decisions, but his team had great respect for his knowledge and expertise. That Supermarine products were the result of his preference for collaborative effort is seen best in the broad variety of designs the team produced and the general lack of a clear 'house style' so typical of many of their competitors.

The three back-to-back Schneider Trophy wins and the numerous air speed records set with his racers lifted Mitchell and Supermarine's status to the premier rank. However, their distinctly lacklustre prototypes of the era and the impact of the depression denied them the opportunity to capitalise on this in the short term and commercial success eluded them. Cash injected into the business by Vickers Aviation (their new owners) and a recruitment drive for staff in Mitchell's design department provided the stimulus the company needed, resulting in two of the company's most successful products in the mid-1930s, the Spitfire and Walrus. It is most regrettable that Mitchell, stricken with incurable cancer in late 1933, was denied the opportunity to see the outstanding contribution to the war effort that his aircraft delivered. He died in the spring of 1937.

Supermarine's aircraft design

The loss of the S4 had been a bitter blow to Mitchell but he was now all too aware that it would have required a fair degree of luck to have won the 1925 contest. It is possible that he had doubts on this score before it had even flown as he had a ⅛-scale model prepared for assessment in the RAE wind tunnels. The report confirming the adverse impact on both lift and drag from the 114 thin tubular vanes in each under-wing Lamblin radiator was in his hands before embarking for the USA. But even prior to reading these results he had set about a complete rethink for his next racer.

BELOW Mitchell's original concept drawings for the S5 produced in November 1925.

The S5 – the foundation for success

It is astounding that Mitchell's first concept drawing for the S5 was produced as early as 17 November 1925, just one day after his return from the USA. We can only assume that the design team had been tasked with developing the idea before he embarked on his outbound trip on 25 September, an indication that he was dissatisfied with the S4 even prior to the contest, despite it having taken the air speed record for marine aircraft. Furthermore, this initial design was far more than just a simple evolution of the S4, although the ancestry could be seen in the lines of the wings and floats. No doubt these drawings were tabled at meetings with the Air Ministry when they met to discuss the possibility for future funding and technical support.

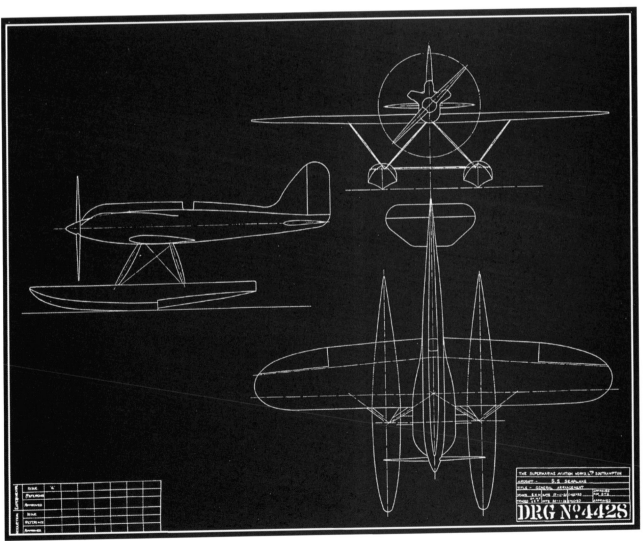

Based on his analysis of the S4's deficiencies, Mitchell had come to three main conclusions: that the frontal cross-section of the aircraft had to be as small as possible, the cantilever wing would be discarded in favour of one with external bracing, and the total wetted area of the aircraft would be reduced. Thus his initial concept was for a low-wing monoplane where the wings and float chassis were braced by outward-canted strut pairs and by lateral struts between the floats, thus creating a rigid Warren girder-type truss. The main fuel tanks were moved from behind the engine to within the floats as this enabled the fuselage to be shortened and the cockpit to be relocated forward over the wing. The top cylinder bank fairing of the tightly cowled Lion engine was extended back to the low-profile cockpit canopy, and the pilot's headrest was at the front of a dorsal spine that blended into the integral fin. The lines of the S5 as eventually built are clear to see right from the initiation of the project.

GAC submitted a design for the all-wood Gloster IV biplane, which paid far greater attention to aerodynamic refinement than had been achieved with the Gloster III; and the Short-Bristow project had a fuselage combining a tubular steel framework at the front and a wooden monocoque to the rear of the cockpit, wire-braced wooden monoplane wings and novel drag-reducing helmet fairings around the radial engine's cylinders. Napier planned

to produce a much-improved Lion for the Supermarine and GAC machines, while Bristol worked on a supercharged racing version of their new Mercury air-cooled radial.

Evaluation of Mitchell's S5 model, alongside those of GAC and Short-Bristow, commenced at the NPL and RAE in March 1926 as soon as the project was formally approved. A ¼-scale model of the S5 had been constructed in mahogany for evaluation in the NPL's 27ft duplex wind tunnel. It came supplied with several movable and alternative parts and differed in detail only from the initial concept drawings, the main exception being the floats which were of a new design. A framework programme of tests had been discussed and agreed in advance between the NPL tunnel technicians, led by William Cowley, and the aircraft designers, that allowed sufficient flexibility for additional investigations to be added should early results indicate that these would be beneficial. This method of a base series of stability, lift and drag tests supplemented by ad hoc investigations suggested by the results proved successful and was continued right through to the work on the S6B in 1931.

In parallel with the extensive wind tunnel programme the floats were to be evaluated in the NPL's William Froude water tank, a channel 500ft long, 30ft wide and 13ft deep along which models could be towed via overhead cradles.

SUPERMARINE'S DESIGN DEPARTMENT

In late 1925, as work on the S5 design commenced, Supermarine's Design Department was of modest size and its primary focus, naturally enough, was on commercial work. Much of this effort was devoted to the new twin-engine Southampton flying boat and its derivatives, the smaller Seamew project, and variants of the Seagull. Work on the S5 had to be accommodated around this. Mitchell's deputy was Frank Holroyd, who had been with the company since the war years, and the senior draughtsman was Joe Smith, employed from Austin Motors in 1921. It may well have been the initiation of the S5 project that prompted Mitchell to split his Design Department into two, with Holroyd running the Technical Office, responsible for stress calculation and aerodynamics, while Smith ran the Drawing Office. Both offices provided ideas to new aircraft designs.

Foremost in the Technical Office were Oliver Simmonds and Alan Clifton, recruited in 1924 and 1923 respectively. Simmonds was a Cambridge engineering graduate, ex-RFC, who had worked at the RAE on wind tunnel evaluations and aircraft inspection. He was an innovative, ambitious and outspoken character and there is little doubt that he would have made a significant contribution to the design of both the S4 and S5. He left Supermarine in 1927 to set up Simmonds Aircraft to produce the Spartan, a light aircraft of his own design, later becoming an MP and establishing a second company, Simmonds Accessories, to manufacture components for the aircraft industry. Clifton was also an engineering graduate employed by Mitchell straight from college to work on stress calculations. He was quieter than Simmonds but an equally valuable asset to the department, whose career would take him to the role of Chief Designer in the 1950s. These two colleagues were the founder members of the Hampshire Aeroplane Club.

Regardless of the technical challenge, design work on the S5 was not restricted to the more experienced members of the team; even the most recent recruits had their opportunity. The very first layout drawing of the S5 was produced by Ernest Mansbridge, a graduate of the University of London, who had been with the company for less than a year. In the letter offering him employment Mitchell had written: 'We should like to point out that you will require considerable instruction both in the drawing office and in the shops before your services will be of any value to us'; Mitchell was certainly providing him with appropriately challenging instruction. Eric Lovell Cooper joined around the same time after completion of an apprenticeship with Boulton and Paul, and it was he who drew the refined layout drawings of the S5 just prior to the initiation of the NPL evaluation. Design of the floats was handled by the hull section in the Drawing Office overseen by Arthur Shirval, much of it the work of George Garrett. Other key drawings were produced by Harold Axtell, Charles 'George' Kettlewell, Dick Laidman, J. Alexander and others. The S5 was very much a team effort and the knowledge they gained through working on the project placed them in an excellent position from which to develop the S6 and S6B. Many would go on to play key roles in the Design Department in the 1930s.

BELOW Supermarine's Design Department was housed in the roof area of the Woolston works. This sketch view was drawn for the department's satirical magazine *The Ragazine* in 1927.

EXIT TRACERS.

Although Supermarine specialised in marine aircraft they had no tank test facilities of their own and there are no records to suggest that they had ever carried out model tests of any kind. The design of the planing bottoms for hulls and floats had been largely a matter of experience and no small amount of luck and Supermarine's products to date had, like those of their competitors, been inconsistent.

Having reviewed the results of the RAE wind tunnel evaluation of the S4 model, and shortly after he had drawn up the preliminary design for the S5, Mitchell requested that they investigate the impact of lowering the wing from mid- to base-fuselage. The results showed that total drag would increase by about 5%, but as the S4 model was rather small-scale and lowering the wing on it had required some rather crude modifications, Mitchell felt that the comparison needed to be repeated on the S5 before he could commit to his design. Therefore he had made sure that the model was built in such a way as to accommodate repositioning of the wings. The NPL results suggested that there was very little variation in drag with the wing placed in various positions below the thrust axis, so Mitchell's preferred layout with the wing at the base of the fuselage was retained and became the norm for his later racers, too. There were sound structural reasons for placing the wing in this position as it freed up space in the fuselage, simplified the method of attachment of the wings and improved the angles for the bracing.

The evaluation of the model then proceeded according to the agreed programme, measuring forces and moments on the whole model, on individual components, and on partial assemblies at various wind speeds up to 100ft/sec. The purpose of the component tests was to assess the contribution that each made to the total drag of the aircraft and to provide an insight into the interference drag inherent in the design. Interference drag was well known to occur between the parts on an aircraft, but had generally received little attention in the assessment of most designs. This was mainly because it was considered of little consequence at the relatively low speeds at which they flew, but the effect certainly could not be ignored for a specialised racer. The results suggested that 30% of the total drag of the model was

attributable to the bracing struts for the floats and wings. Mitchell had anticipated this and so the model was rebuilt with all the bracing struts removed and replaced by wires of streamline section. However, when this revised model was tested the drag was found to be little different and the problem appeared to be attributable to the difficulty in fabricating streamline wires accurately to scale and then aligning them on the model at the correct angle of incidence. The matter was further confused when examples of full-scale streamlined wires were evaluated in the 4ft wind tunnel and proved to generate slightly higher drag than wires of simple lenticular section. Although this was counter-intuitive it was decided to use lenticular wires on the aircraft while the reasons for the unexpected wind tunnel results were reviewed. As the struts had been shown to contribute a large percentage of the total drag, the four in the float chassis were singled out for further tests with revised streamline section. Measurements indicated that an improvement in their drag of as much as 30% would be possible by adopting the revised profile.

To complete the investigation a number of alterations and substitute parts were evaluated. Mitchell was unsure how the prominent lateral cylinder banks of the Lion engine should best be faired into the fuselage sides and he provided tail fairings of three different lengths. There was negligible change in drag so the median length was adopted as this provided sufficient internal volume to accommodate the fuel header tank without an undue reduction in the view for the pilot. In order to improve the forward view through the canopy the side panels were angled inwards slightly and the fairing to the rear of the central cylinder bank narrowed accordingly. The dorsal spine behind the pilot's headrest on the model was also reduced in width and the side profile, originally slightly arched, was planed straight, possibly a precursor to Mitchell's decision to lengthen the rear fuselage slightly.

While work was under way in the wind tunnels the floats were subject to test in the water tank. Pairs of ⅛-scale floats and struts were towed in the tank at speeds of up to 34kts and photographed to assess how cleanly they ran and how their intersecting bow waves would impact on the propeller at the front and the tailplane at the rear, both represented by wire frames. The volume of the floats was dictated by the total weight of the aircraft and the amount of reserve buoyancy that was deemed acceptable. For a regular military or commercial seaplane the reserve buoyancy was typically 90 to 100%, that is to say that the floats were capable of supporting twice the weight of the aircraft, while for the S4 floats it had been 68%. Mitchell felt that this could be reduced further to 50% for the S5. The floats were required to be stable at all speeds on the water, during which the aircraft was accelerating, the running angle was changing, and the load slowly decreasing as wing lift increased. It is important to realise that the take-off speed of the aircraft was higher than the current water speed record.

A preliminary design, Model A, had proven very good in the wind tunnel but unacceptable in the tank as the nose had a tendency to dive below the water surface, and so had to be discarded. A redesigned float, Model B, was used to evaluate seven different modifications

in position of the step and profile, with varying success, and the results were then used to guide a further redesign. This was Model C which, after adjustment to the position of the step, was accepted as the final version for construction. Some of these tests were re-run late in the programme after the design of the aircraft had been refined. The spacing between the floats had been modified and the position of the centre of gravity of the aircraft moved forward and slightly to one side. No particular problems were identified, although water was prone to impact first on the propeller and then the tailplane as the aircraft accelerated.

The complete S5 model was then assessed for lift and drag in yaw at the angles of incidence corresponding to maximum speed and at the stall, which established the stability of the aircraft.

At the RAE measurements were made of the heat dissipation capability for a section of the S5's water radiators. Mitchell had adopted surface radiators on the wings, as had proven so successful by Curtiss, but wished to have a smooth rather than corrugated outer surface.

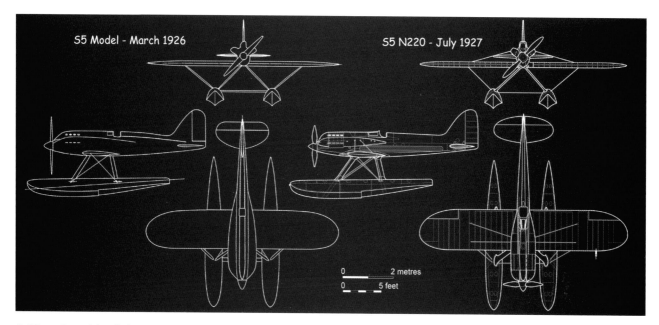

S5 Model - March 1926   S5 N220 - July 1927

0   2 metres
0   5 feet

A 5ft section of the S5's wooden wing was mounted in the 7ft wind tunnel with portions of the flat-surface copper radiator attached to top and bottom. Heated water was passed through the radiators at the rate expected from the water pumps of the Lion engine and at a temperature around 67°C above the inlet air temperature in the tunnel. The temperature of the water entering and exiting the radiators was measured at various air speeds up to 110ft/sec and at various angles of incidence, from which the cooling capacity at racing speeds could be estimated. However, it was acknowledged that extrapolating to air speeds some four times that in the wind tunnel was likely to be prone to error. Tests were also carried out with the radiator painted first with aluminium paint and then with black. Both improved the cooling efficiency but surprisingly aluminium was the better of the two, which was felt to be attributable to the change in surface texture. No evaluation was made of the corrugated oil coolers that were to be placed on the fuselage sides.

The NPL tests had demonstrated that Mitchell's base design was sound and had indicated areas where small improvement may have been possible. In addition it had highlighted the problems inherent in manufacturing a scale model in wood to a high degree of accuracy and subsequently of assembling this in the wind tunnel with all components at the correct orientation. Warping of thinner parts of the wooden model was encountered from the start

and small components, such as the wires, proved problematic. Nevertheless Mitchell was able to progress with construction of the S5 confident that it was unlikely to encounter significant problems, and this was indeed the case.

The wind tunnel evaluation of the Gloster IV had resulted in significant changes in design, notably for the wings, while that for the Crusader had shown that reducing the drag of a radial engine by fitting helmets (or cowls) of various shapes to the cylinders was largely ineffective, even before the impact on engine cooling was taken into consideration. It was found that the drag of the fuselage with engine and cowls in place was roughly equal to that of the whole S5 model.

A comparison of the final S5 against the model evaluated by the NPL shows that the changes were numerous but relatively minor. The wing plan had been modified to constant chord, presumably to simplify construction and to facilitate installation of the radiators, and the tailplane was now of elliptical plan. The rear fuselage had been lengthened slightly. The only modification to the shape of the aircraft resulting from the flight-test programme was a small re-contouring of the cylinder bank nose fairings to improve the internal flow of cooling air.

After the conclusion of the development test flights and the 1927 contest, a fair amount of direct measurements of the aircraft's performance was available to supplement the NPL and RAE model research. Mitchell was able

ABOVE The final Supermarine Napier S5 differed only in detail from the model tested by the NPL.

to summarise what had been learned. His key aim had been to produce an aircraft that was significantly smaller than the S4 and had resulted in the structural weight of the S5 amounting to just 36% of the total aircraft compared to 45% for the S4. By tailoring the fuselage cross section tightly around the engine and moving away from classic 'airship' form a reduction of nearly 40% had been achieved, and for the smaller floats the reduction was 14%. The surface area of the fuselage had been reduced by over 30% and of the floats by 10%. The wind tunnel tests suggested that the total interference drag between components amounted to 17.5% of the total, most of which was attributable to the bracing wires. In conclusion Mitchell assessed the improvement in top speed that had been achieved in comparison to the S4 and concluded that it could be broken down as follows:

- ■ Wire bracing of wings and floats   +5mph
- ■ Smaller floats   +4mph
- ■ Smaller fuselage   +11mph
- ■ Flat surface radiators   +24mph
- ■ Increase in engine power and
  gearing   +30mph
- ■ Lowering wing   -3mph.

After the 1927 Schneider Trophy contest had been run the research programme was effectively terminated, although some further evaluation of the Gloster IV suggested by the early work continued at the NPL with modest Air Ministry support. With no government funding for aircraft to compete in the 1928 contest costs were scaled back accordingly, so with limited time and funds Supermarine planned to undertake

no more than a simple modification of the S5 in order to accommodate Napier's Lion VIIC, a higher-revving version of the VIIB that they expected to deliver 1,000hp. Mitchell's preliminary calculations suggested that the strengthening of the aircraft structure would only raise the weight by around 150lb, but the resultant increase in top speed was likely to be less than 10mph. As the S5 had differed in a number of ways from the model tested in the NPL wind tunnel Mitchell had a new one prepared for evaluation, but when the Air Ministry reversed its decision on funding he was able to consider a completely new aircraft design incorporating all that he had learned from the extensive research and flight-testing of the S5.

In conjunction with his assessment of the factors responsible for the S5's 70mph speed advantage over the S4, Mitchell produced a simple chart to illustrate how the most effective methods to raise speed were by increasing engine power and reducing resistance. Yet it was clear from the evaluation of the S5 that the improvement in resistance that had been achieved was due largely to the reduction in cross section of the fuselage and floats, and these would be difficult to reduce further as their size was dictated by the dimensions of the engine and pilot, and by the necessary reserve buoyancy of the floats. It appeared that the key to major speed gains would have to come from a substantial increase in engine power. When government support was restored Rolls-Royce agreed to provide such an engine – the 'Racing H', later renamed the 'R' – and would work with Supermarine exclusively so that the engine and airframe could be developed together.

The S6 – refining the racing line

Mitchell and his team had conceived the lines of the S5 in the autumn of 1925 and no significant change to the layout had been suggested from the extensive wind tunnel evaluation in 1926. It was a sound design from the outset; the aircraft performed extremely well and was preferred by all the pilots to the Gloster IV. The inquiry into Kinkead's crash in the third S5 was never published, thus leaving plenty of scope for speculation, but it is fair

BELOW Refined packaging of the engine ancillaries and a fuselage design tailored around it led to a dramatic reduction in the frontal cross section.

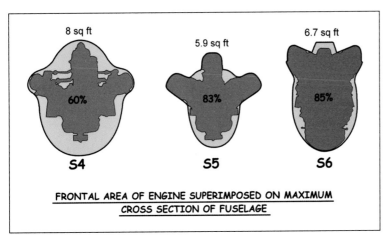

FRONTAL AREA OF ENGINE SUPERIMPOSED ON MAXIMUM CROSS SECTION OF FUSELAGE

S4 — 8 sq ft — 60%
S5 — 5.9 sq ft — 83%
S6 — 6.7 sq ft — 85%

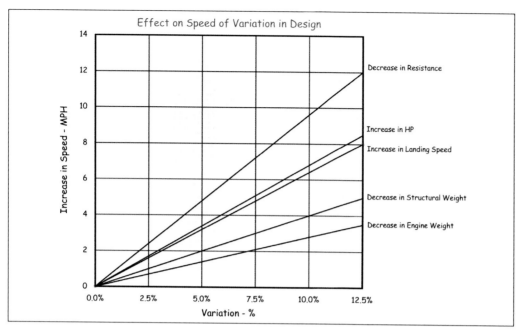

Effect on Speed of Variation in Design

Decrease in Resistance
Increase in HP
Increase in Landing Speed
Decrease in Structural Weight
Decrease in Engine Weight

Increase in Speed - MPH

Variation - %

LEFT Mitchell's simple chart, based on the S5, shows how he thought changes to various elements would affect top speed and why he focussed on increased engine power for the S6.

to assume that no fault was found with the S5 as the remaining two aircraft were flown extensively, including high-g turns, racing and speed record attempts, all without modification. As a consequence Mitchell saw no need to deviate far from its key characteristics when commencing design of the S6, and hence there was a strong family resemblance. The tail surfaces and wing plan in particular were all very similar. The new 'R' engine, at 36 litres, was going to be far larger than the 27-litre Lion VIIB, especially in length as it was a V12 with two banks of six cylinders, compared to the Lion's three banks of four, and was fitted with a substantial supercharger at the rear. The simple spur gearing gave the engine a higher thrust line. It would also weigh more than 1,500lb, which was over half as much again as the Lion, and this meant that the cantilever engine mount of the S5 was no longer appropriate and the positioning of the wing and float chassis struts would need to be revised to accommodate the load.

The NPL wind tunnel tests of the S6 took over from where they had left off with the previous S5-based model and repeated the earlier tests. A basic set of force and moment measurements were run on the whole model, but these were little more than a formality as much of the S5 data was applicable given the close similarity of the aircraft. There then started the tricky matter of finding an

acceptable compromise float design, balancing hydrodynamic and aerodynamic performance, in association with the William Froude water tank. As Supermarine were now wholly owned by Vickers they also had access to that company's hull development water tanks at St Albans and so were able to run additional tests of their own.

Two important areas of new research to be undertaken at the NPL were an assessment of the aerodynamic interference between the floats and the main aircraft and the implications of compression effects on drag. The former was necessary as the heavier aircraft would require substantially larger floats and there was a desire to minimise the height of the aircraft to keep the centre of gravity low for reasons of stability; the latter had been discussed during work on the S5 and some preliminary studies had been made by sharpening the leading edge of the wing, but it was known that this was of little value as the highest speed attainable in the wind tunnel was well below that at which compression effects would become noticeable.

There is nothing to suggest that the floats on the S5 had been noticeably poor either on the water or in the air, but rather than build upon the design experience developing them Mitchell started afresh for the S6. The key aim was to derive a profile with far lower drag in the air while perhaps accepting some sacrifice in performance on the water in the process. This research used an iterative approach,

RIGHT This ¼-scale mahogany model of the S6 was used for evaluation in the wind tunnel. The thin wings were difficult to construct accurately to scale and were prone to warping.
(Crown Copyright)

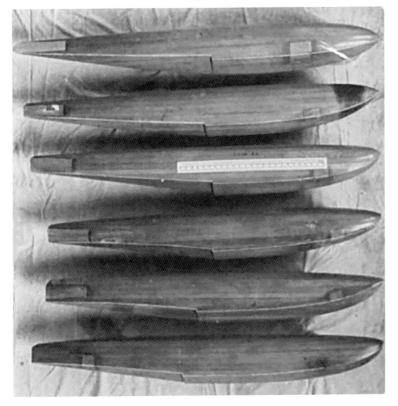

BELOW Many float designs were evaluated for the S6 in order to derive the best compromise between hydrodynamic performance and aerodynamic drag.
(Crown Copyright)

commencing with a float approximating 'airship' form with a basic planing bottom and the appropriate reserve buoyancy. This design, which, as expected, had very poor hydrodynamic performance, was modified progressively after each test run in the wind tunnel and water tank to reach an acceptable compromise, but it proved to be surprisingly difficult. The early modified designs showed a distinct tendency to dive below the surface at low speed, which would have made take-off and coming to a stop after landing hazardous, but eventually six designs were considered worthy of further work. These were evaluated in the wind tunnel for drag at a range of angles of attack and with a variety of modifications such as fairing the step and extending the sides downwards at the chines. The final selected design had a slightly lower reserve buoyancy and greater water drag than those on the S5 but the air drag was notably better, a 10% improvement in drag in terms of frontal area and of displacement. Mitchell, however, was still concerned about the possibility of the noses diving and produced an alternative version with a raised bow as a precaution. In a paper written in 1930 Mitchell noted that the torque of the 'R' engine amounted to 5,700ft/lb and that this had the effect of adding a load of 750lb, a 30% increase, to the port float and a corresponding decrease on the starboard. It was obvious, he said with the benefit of hindsight, that provision should have been made to represent this in the tank tests.

To minimise the length of the drag-inducing float chassis struts and to lower the centre of gravity of the aircraft, Mitchell wished to mount the floats closer to the wings than on the S5, but he needed to see how far they could be raised without running into interference drag problems. He also needed to find the optimum angle at which to mount the floats relative to the thrust line. Wind tunnel tests were carried out with the floats mounted at various heights between the equivalent of +1.33 and –1.33ft from the preferred position, and these confirmed that the planned position was indeed the best. Similar tests angled the floats between +4° and –4° relative to the fuselage datum, and these showed that a negative angle of –3.75° resulted in the lowest drag.

Mitchell was aware that there was limited potential for improvement in resistance through a reduction in profile cross section or surface area, so more attention was paid to surface details. Each successive S5 aircraft had seen an improvement over the previous example as the skill of the metalworkers grew, and the increasing use of flush riveting was particularly noticeable. As this was a laborious process a study was initiated to see how beneficial it had been. A ⅛-scale float left over from the evaluation of the Crusader in 1927 was used as the test model. Measurements of drag were made for this smooth float over a range of speeds in the 7ft wind tunnel. The model was then modified to approximate how it may have looked with dome head rivets with a head diameter of ¼in and standing proud of the surface by ⅛in, which had to be reproduced at scale. It was estimated that the float would have around 7,000 rivets. Grooves were cut into the float model where the lines of rivets were likely to have been placed and these were filled with Plasticine modelling clay. Into this were inserted small silvered sugar-ball cake decorations that were found to be roughly the size required to simulate the rivet heads. The drag tests were then re-run and the results showed an increase of 40% compared to the smooth float and this, at full scale on the S5, could have resulted in an increase in top speed of 10mph had their floats been totally smooth.

Later the opportunity arose to be able to compare these model results with an evaluation at full-scale when two S5 floats became available, one with dome head riveting throughout and the other with a substantial amount of flush riveting. However, the flush-riveted float still had dome rivets for the fuel tank mid-section and the many access panels had screw heads standing proud of the surface, so much time was spent adding filler and patches to smooth these over. The drag tests were then run in the 7ft wind tunnel, with measurements showing that the dome-head-riveted float generated only 14% more drag than the smooth version. The marked difference between these results and those for the model was attributed to the fact that the smoothed float was far less smooth than the model, that there was a scale effect to take into account and that the amount of turbulence in the tunnel was probably different for the two evaluations due to the large size of the full-size float. In combination the studies demonstrated the importance of achieving the smoothest possible surface on the aircraft, although there were still questions about how much improvement in top speed could be achieved.

The wind tunnel study of bracing wire profiles from the 1927 programme was re-run as the results had proven counter-intuitive. These tests had suggested that simple lenticular wires generated less drag than aerofoil sections. A repeat of the evaluation using bracing wires with an improved aerofoil section and fabricated to a higher standard was indeed proven to be superior to lenticular wires, and henceforward it was adopted for the S6.

A suggestion that exhaust gases from the engine could have a detrimental impact on drag was assessed by taking the old S5 fuselage model, drilling holes at the positions of the exhaust stubs and connecting these to a compressed air supply. No appreciable change in drag was noted.

The question of drag rise due to air compression at high speed had been raised on a number of occasions, most especially with regard to the propellers, but it was now becoming of significance for the aircraft itself as the planned top speed was approaching 350mph. Although this was still only half the speed of sound at sea level it was a possible issue that could no longer be ignored as the local airflow around parts of the aircraft would be significantly higher. Mitchell intended to specify a thinner aerofoil profile for the S6 wing rather than the 12.6% t/c RAF30 (t/c = thickness/chord ratio, which is the maximum thickness of the aerofoil expressed as a percentage of the chord) that had been used on both the S4 and S5. He selected RAF27, which had a t/c of 9.8%. The NPL also wished to compare both of these profiles against the NACA M (National Advisory Committee on Aeronautics, aerofoil M), which had a t/c of 8%. Model wings were constructed at ¼ scale for each aerofoil section for assessment in the wind tunnel. It proved to be very difficult to produce accurate thin profiles in wood and warping was a problem, one wing having to be rejected and replaced. At the low air velocities that could be achieved in the tunnel there was little to choose between the three and Mitchell decided to stay with RAF27 as its lift at moderate angles of attack was superior and thus beneficial at take-off and landing. Observations of the S5 when landing and at take-off had shown that the nose of the aircraft had to be held unreasonably high in order to maintain lift.

In addition to these evaluations a further investigation was initiated using the 3in section high-speed jet wind tunnel, capable of air speeds well in excess of Mach 1, which had recently been installed at the NPL and run personally by the superintendent of the Engineering Department, Sir Thomas Stanton. Wing models were prepared in metal with aerofoils of RAF30 and RAF27 and also of the same profiles modified with sharpened leading edges. These were evaluated at Mach 0.35 and Mach 0.5, the speed range at which the S6 would race, and it was found that the minimum drag of both aerofoils was reduced by sharpening the leading edge. However, drag increased at higher angles of attack for RAF30 and the lift of RAF27 was reduced by the modification. Comparing these results with those from the 27ft wind tunnel at lower speeds suggested that compression effects were indeed coming into play towards the maximum speed of the aircraft, although the accuracy of the results from the experimental high-speed jet were questionable as repeated tests often provided significantly different results.

Although the construction of the S6's wing surface water radiators was to be quite different from those fitted to the S5, both had flat exterior surfaces. As such no additional evaluation of cooling capacity appears to have been carried out at the RAE, although a test section had been provided to them, possibly for strength testing. However, the fuselage-mounted corrugated oil coolers used on the S5 had not been tested prior to construction and these radiators had to be substantially augmented after the early flight-tests showed the cooling surfaces to be inadequate. For the S6 Mitchell intended to install coolers of similar form and to supplement these by utilising the oil tank outer surfaces, so the efficiency of the whole system needed to be proven. Mitchell had designed the S6's fin as the aircraft's oil tank, to be built as an integral part of the fuselage. Corrugated coolers ran along both sides of the fuselage and were simply enlarged versions of those that had proven successful on the S5. A further corrugated cooler ran along the base of the fuselage to return the oil to the engine. Supermarine provided a fin tank for evaluation in the RAE's 7ft wind tunnel, and this was installed with the portions that would normally be enclosed within the fuselage, suitably insulated from the airflow. Oil was sprayed on to the interior surface of the fin by one of two methods: a Carter centrifuger – a rotating sprayer that functioned in a similar manner to a garden sprinkler – and a simple closed tube with perforations of various sizes. Oil was passed through the system at a rate of 6.3 to 6.7gals/min at an inlet temperature of 90 to 93°C. For the second test spare oil coolers from the S5 were fitted along the sides of the only convenient fuselage that the RAE had available, which happened to be that of the Gloster VI provided by GAC for assessment of its own oil cooling system.

Rolls-Royce had indicated that the total heat that the oil cooling system would need to dissipate was the equivalent of 47hp. The wind tunnel tests, extrapolated to contest speeds, suggested cooling capacity at around 19hp for the tank and 16hp for the two 11ft S5 corrugated coolers. It was noted that the dissipation measured for the corrugated coolers, the only oil radiator surfaces on the S5, was just under half the 33hp that Napier said had been required for the Lion, yet there had been no problems experienced during the testing, contest or subsequent flights. The reasons for this discrepancy remained unexplained but it was suggested that the method for extrapolating wind tunnel measurements to the higher speeds of the aircraft underestimated the cooling capacity under flight conditions. However, as Mitchell had designed the side coolers on the S6 to have around twice the cooling surface of those on the S5 (and there was the additional surface of the corrugated ventral fuselage cooler also to consider), the cooling capacity was considered to be adequate and flight-tests would prove this to be so.

During early bench runs of the Rolls-Royce 'R' engine there were serious concerns about the rate of oil consumption and whether the S6's tank would be of sufficient size to hold the volume required for the duration of the contest. This, combined with uncertainty regarding the cooling capacity of the system, led Mitchell's team to draw up a fall-back scheme whereby a 5ft 6in length of the rear fuselage would be sealed off to form a large oil tank, with the original fin tank now functioning as a cooler only. The flight control cables would pass through the tank, contained within tubes. Thankfully Rolls-Royce made considerable progress dealing with oil consumption and there was no need for the radical change.

In early flight-tests of the S6 it was found that the cooling provided by the wing surface water radiators was quite inadequate and the engine could not be run at maximum revs. The idea was proposed of allowing the engine to run at higher temperatures by using ethylene glycol as the coolant, but this was soon abandoned as unacceptable. Mitchell dealt with the problem in two ways: first, by adding air scoops under the wing tips and vents in the upper surface at the root to allow the inner surface of the radiators between the spars to receive a cooling airflow; and, secondly, by adding flat-surface radiators as 'patches' on the floats. At the same time he took the opportunity to replace the starboard float with the version featuring a longer and raised nose, because the aircraft had turned out to be overweight and sat lower in the water than planned and was prone to porpoising. Prior to the 1929 contest neither of these modifications had been evaluated in the wind tunnel as there was insufficient time.

The S6 as built hardly differed from the model tested in the wind tunnel. Mitchell's experience with the S5 had served him well and no changes had been necessary during detailed design. There is no doubt that the S6 was a successful aircraft – it won the Schneider Trophy in 1929 and established a new absolute world air speed record, but it had been a close-run thing. The aircraft's performance on the water, exacerbated by worrying weight increases, had given cause for concern and even with the additional float patches the combined radiator area was still not able to cool the water sufficiently to allow the engine to be run at full throttle for extended periods.

BELOW The Supermarine Rolls-Royce S6 was virtually unchanged from the model tested by the NPL, a testimony to the experience gained from design and development of the S5.

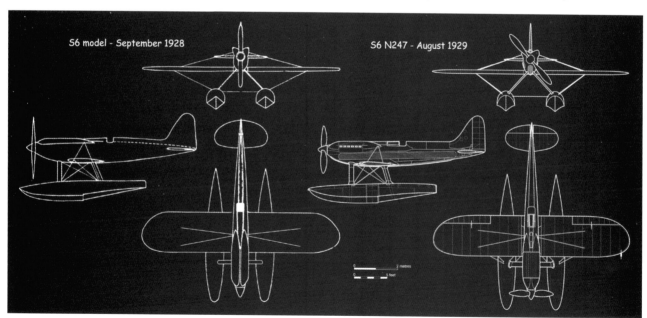

S6 model - September 1928

S6 N247 - August 1929

Mitchell's analysis of the work supporting the S6 design showed that many of the issues identified on the S5 had remained largely unchanged despite the extensive research. The wire bracing still accounted for nearly 20% of the total drag and a major proportion of this was due to interference with other parts of the aircraft. Despite a concerted effort to improve the aerodynamic drag of the floats the improvement had not been dramatic, and it came at the expense of seriously degraded water performance. The reduction in drag that had been achieved was then eroded by the need to attach external radiators and by the raising of the nose of the substitute starboard floats.

The S6B – the 'eleventh-hour' racer

After the 1929 contest the government once again cancelled all further funding for Schneider Trophy racing and cut back drastically on the high-speed aircraft research programme. A little work continued at the RAE to assess the benefit of the internal wing cooling system applied in haste to the S6, and some limited flying of the aircraft took place at the MAEE, where a skeleton HSF was based, to evaluate how well the wind tunnel results and other studies had predicted their performance, although this work focussed mostly on the S5 and Gloster IV. There are no records to suggest that Mitchell carried out any new studies on racer design, no potential S7, until the dramatic turnaround at the very end of January 1931 when Lady Houston underwrote the entire cost of preparing new racers. With little time and funds barely sufficient to build aircraft, Mitchell prepared to construct two new S6 airframes, unchanged from 1929 apart from local strengthening and a larger fin oil tank. The floats, however, did need further development.

The S6 floats had barely sufficed: they were overloaded and the last-minute replacement starboard floats were a quick-fix but a poor compromise. One change to the contest rules that had been proposed by the RAeC and passed by the FAI was to replace the navigability and mooring trials held on the day prior to the main contest with a landing and taxiing test, which would take place just prior to entering the speed course. This entailed landing and then taxiing at moderate speed while carrying the full fuel load and obviously required careful thought in the design of the floats.

It had been agreed that the two original S6s would be refurbished and fitted with new floats that were basically the 1929 design, lengthened fore and aft to improve buoyancy. Water radiators were attached to the nose top decking and the sides, but these were not tested for their cooling capacity. The modified aircraft, an insurance against late delivery of the new type, were referred to as S6A. Work was then put in hand at the NPL to design completely revised floats for the new aircraft, to be called S6B.

Once more Mitchell started with new designs of increased length and six were prepared for full tests, including that destined for the S6A, in the Vickers test-tanks and the NPL wind tunnel. To tackle the poor performance experienced with the S6 on the water one set of floats proposed for the S6B were considerably longer than the others and of slightly reduced cross section. A lot of time was spent refining the nose sections as this seemed to be the more critical from the point of view of aerodynamic drag. As floats were eliminated one by one the remaining options had small vertical extensions added to the sides, projecting down about 1in full-scale at the chine. These were applied to the forward part of the float running from a couple of feet behind the bow back to the step, the portion where the plan profile was roughly parallel. These were intended to improve performance on the water by constraining the bow wave and reducing the interference between the two floats, although at the expense of some additional drag in the air. The idea had first been tested on model floats in 1927 and again in 1929, but had been rejected both times as air drag increased on some models by as much as 10%, but in the light of the difficulties experienced on the water in 1929 the compromise had to be accepted.

Having tested so many alternative float designs, not just from Supermarine but also those from Gloster and Short, the NPL looked for some simple mathematical model to express the relative efficiency of floats in general. On the assumption, almost certainly misplaced, that all performed equally on the water they

RIGHT Efficient float design proved elusive and was still largely a matter of trial and error, but improvement was noticeable. Here, the decrease in water drag during acceleration is shown for three designs.

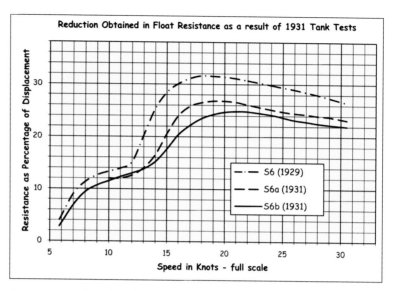

Reduction Obtained in Float Resistance as a result of 1931 Tank Tests

Resistance as Percentage of Displacement / Speed in Knots - full scale

S6 (1929)
S6a (1931)
S6b (1931)

concentrated on aerodynamic qualities. A 'Figure of Merit' was derived by dividing the minimum air drag at 100ft/sec by the ⅔ power of the volume. On this basis the best were deemed to be those produced by Short Bros, with a design for use on the Gloster VI topping the ranking, and the one for the Short-Bristow Crusader close behind. One of Mitchell's designs for the S6B followed and the NPL felt that its performance could have been improved further by lowering the nose slightly, but this suggestion was rejected by Mitchell as it could have increased the chances of the float diving.

After the initial attempts to take off in the S6B had to be aborted, and the aircraft was subsequently fitted with a modified 1929 propeller in order to achieve flight, there followed hurried discussions between Supermarine and Fairey. The complex issue of how the propeller's slipstream affected drag, stability and control surface effectiveness resulted in the NPL initiating a programme of tests with the aircraft model fitted with a propeller driven by an electric motor. These wind tunnel tests with the model mounted at the angle of attack representative of take-off conditions replicated the observations from flight-testing, and showed how the more concentrated slipstream from the small-diameter propeller produced a stronger yaw moment than the larger designs. This was due in some measure to its impact on the fin and rudder, partly because of the asymmetric thrust from the rising and descending blades of the propeller, which had its axis of rotation about 12° from the airflow, and partly because of the complex interaction of the slipstream with the water surface.

Stability problems in yaw during flight that were later attributed to the helical slipstream impacting adversely on the fin and rudder had been experienced on the Gloster IVA and IVB, both of which had fins and rudders that were symmetrical above and below the thrust line. When the aircraft were reconfigured as trainers these were replaced by the more conventional design from the Gloster IV, which was entirely above the thrust line, and this alleviated much of the problem. The S5 and S6 both had their fins above the thrust line from the start and did not suffer such noticeable problems, but from the model tests it was found that the S6B's propeller slipstream had a destabilising effect at high wind speeds and low incidence representative of racing conditions, but conversely stabilising at lower speeds and high angle of attack, as at take-off.

BELOW Fairey's calculation of slipsteam twist show why the small-diameter propeller on the S6B caused serious handling problems on the water.

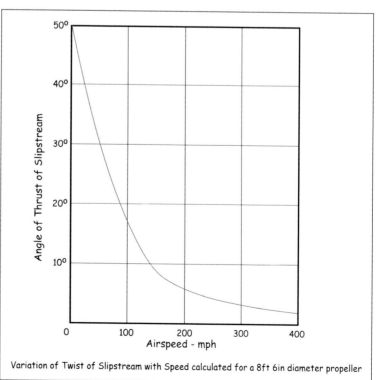

Angle of Thrust of Slipstream / Airspeed - mph

Variation of Twist of Slipstream with Speed calculated for a 8ft 6in diameter propeller

Chapter Three

The engine development programme

Many factors determine the success or otherwise of a racing aircraft, but of paramount importance is the power and reliability of the engine. Although it was the work of Rolls-Royce that ultimately secured the Schneider Trophy for Britain in 1931, the dominant force for many years was Napier.

OPPOSITE The Rolls-Royce 'R' engine was subject to exhaustive development in the test shed. In this staged photograph members of the test staff look on – but the engine is clearly not running.

Napier

The Napier Lion was a 27-litre, 12-cylinder water-cooled engine of 'W' or broad-arrow configuration, with three banks of four cylinders. Lions had powered both the Fairey N10 and the Supermarine Sea Lion in the 1919 Schneider Trophy contest and also the line of GAC landplane racers. It was a robust and reliable engine, failures were rare and as a consequence the Lion soon earned itself an enviable reputation. Supermarine were certainly impressed and they chose to have the Lion installed in the company's Seagull, Swan and Southampton flying boats, and, in race-tuned form, in the Sea Lion II that won the Schneider Trophy in 1922 and the following year's Sea Lion III.

In 1924 Napier worked with GAC to develop a specialised racing Lion of 615hp for their Gloster II seaplane, which was effectively the prototype for the Series VII, the first Lion designed specifically to be installed in the streamlined fuselage of a racing aircraft. This entailed moving the carburettors and other ancillaries to the rear to provide a cleaner nose to the engine. Unfortunately the Gloster II was wrecked but the Lion design was refined further and selected for both the Gloster III and Supermarine S4 seaplanes for the 1925 contest.

The Napier Lion VII produced 680hp compared to the 450hp of the standard engine and this was comfortably above the 500hp or so that the Curtiss D-12 was thought to deliver in racing form. The combination of a dedicated racing engine and airframes constructed with a degree of Air Ministry financial support led many to believe that the British team would stand a good chance of success in the contest, but accidents left them with just a single Gloster III, which could not come close to the speeds of the US aircraft. It was, however, a close-run thing as two of the three Curtiss aircraft suffered engine failure while the Lion performed flawlessly.

In the aftermath of the contest there was a great deal of debate in Britain as to the reasons for failure and for the superiority of the US racers, but all agreed that Napier had done sterling service and that the Lion had performed without fault. After the Air Ministry agreed to fund the high-speed aircraft research programme, further development of the Lion was included within this.

One factor on which there was broad agreement was that the frontal cross section of the Curtiss racer was considerably less than that of the Gloster and Supermarine and this was, in part, a consequence of the broad-arrow layout of the Lion compared to the V12 configuration of the Curtiss. Nevertheless the Lion was still the preferred racing engine – there being no serious alternative, in fact – and efforts were made to slim it down. An 'ideal' fuselage was drawn up and modelled by Napier to act as a guide for the revision of the engine. Napier's designers, led by Capt Nicholson, resolved to reduce the cross section by a careful re-routing of pipework to nestle snugly against the crankcase, and by a radical redesign of the cylinders to reduce their height. This was achieved without affecting the stroke by shortening both the piston crowns and the connecting rods, by raising the compression from 8:1 to 10:1, and by designing a more compact camshaft and valve arrangement. A total reduction in height of 2in was achieved for each cylinder row.

There had been some theoretical work carried out by the RAE into the implications of decreasing the weight of rotating and reciprocating components in an engine, concentrating on bearing loads and gas velocities, but otherwise it appears that Napier developed the engine without direct technical support. However, they were heavily dependent on the companies that supplied magnetos, spark plugs and other components to produce products capable of operating at the higher pressures, temperatures and revolutions required for a racing engine.

The shape of the cylinder head covers were tailored to match the contours of the S5 and Gloster IV and left exposed to the airflow without cowling to aid cooling. The engine was produced in two forms, a standard 910hp direct-drive version and a second, delivering 875hp, which employed a layshaft for gearing, an arrangement that allowed the propeller shaft to remain coaxial with the crankshaft. The two engine types, named VIIA and VIIB respectively, were thus interchangeable within the airframe. Special fuel had to be blended to meet the demands of the high-compression engine.

Very few problems were encountered with either version of the engine, although both Supermarine and GAC had to add more cooling surface for the oil and Supermarine cut small scoops into the nose of the S5 to aid in cooling the engine crankcase and cylinders. During the contest Kinkead's Gloster IVB developed a severe vibration and he was forced to throttle back and retire. When examined later the propeller shaft was found to have cracked, a

very rare failure for a Lion, and was likely to have sheared completely had he continued to race.

For the 1928 contest Napier first proposed the Lion VIIC, a direct derivative of the VIIB designed to produce 1,000hp primarily by increasing engine revs, but when it was agreed that the contest would shift to 1929 these plans were shelved. The additional 12 months was sufficient to allow new designs of engines to be considered, so Napier decided to add

ABOVE The nose of the Supermarine Napier S5 was dominated by the close-cowled Lion engine in the cantilever mount.

LEFT A Napier Lion VIIB geared engine destined for the S5. The cylinder head camshaft covers were specially shaped to the aircraft profile and left exposed to the slipstream to aid cooling.

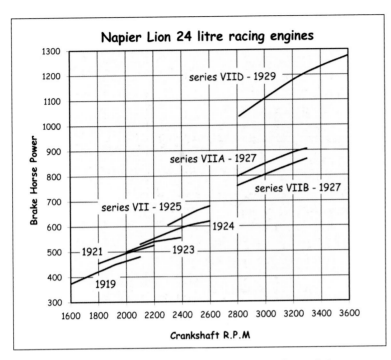

Napier Lion 24 litre racing engines

series VIID - 1929

series VIIA - 1927

series VIIB - 1927

series VII - 1925

1924

1921

1923

1919

Brake Horse Power (vertical axis): 300, 400, 500, 600, 700, 800, 900, 1000, 1100, 1200, 1300

Crankshaft R.P.M (horizontal axis): 1600 1800 2000 2200 2400 2600 2800 3000 3200 3400 3600

ABOVE The increase in power output that Napier achieved with the Lion was dramatic but Mitchell wanted more for the S6 and looked elsewhere.

supercharging to a further slimmed-down evolution of the Lion VIIB, and the new VIID was expected to deliver over 1,250hp. Mitchell, however, felt that even more power would be necessary to remain competitive, so he was seeking something more potent and cast his eyes in the direction of Rolls-Royce.

Rolls-Royce

In the early 1920s Curtiss were by far the dominant force in air racing. Their land racers had flown in the Pulitzer Prize races in the US and had set several speed records, all of which was known in Britain and well reported in the aviation press. Yet it was only when the Curtiss CR-3s arrived in Britain for the 1923 Schneider contest that the British aircraft industry really sat up and took notice. While the consequences of the Curtiss' victory were sinking in Richard Fairey set out to meet Curtiss management and negotiate manufacturing licences for the D-12 engine and the Curtiss-Reed metal propellers. These were installed in his private venture Fox light bomber in early 1925, which caused an immediate controversy in Britain. Fairey's acquisition of the rights to produce the engine flew in the face of well-established Air Ministry policy to promote only British engine designs and to specify as such for military aircraft. They did not welcome a new engine manufacturer

building foreign-designed products and did not support his venture either politically or financially. However, 30 D-12s were ordered from Curtiss for evaluation and installation in a single squadron of Fox bombers, so although his business decisions were distinctly ill-judged he did at least have the consolation of a small aircraft production contract. The two British manufacturers of large water-cooled aircraft engines, Napier and Rolls-Royce, were then actively encouraged by the Air Ministry to assess the Curtiss engines and to come up with something better of their own. Napier declined, believing that the Lion still had plenty of years of development potential ahead of it, while Rolls-Royce gave the opportunity some thought.

The board of Rolls-Royce had long been divided on the whole matter of aircraft engine production, many wishing to concentrate on their range of prestige motor cars irrespective of the company having built a strong reputation for aircraft engines with the Eagle, Falcon and Condor. These three had continued in small-scale production in the early 1920s but no new designs had been authorised. However, when they were approached by the Air Ministry the opportunity to produce a new design adopting the best features of the D-12 received the support of Henry Royce, and the board accepted the decision. The project to develop a completely new engine producing over 500hp was placed in the hands of Arthur Rowledge, coincidently the chief designer of the Napier Lion and now one of Royce's key deputies, and the company initiated a recruitment drive for young university educated engineers to bolster their Experimental Department, run by Ernest Hives. The outcome of this design work was the V12 'F', later named Kestrel, which had a displacement of 21 litres and an initial output of 500hp with plenty of potential for more. After a slightly shaky start the engine went into production in early 1927 and set the aircraft engine division on course for renewed commercial success. In late 1927 it was decided to produce a bigger engine primarily for use in large flying boats by a simple up-scaling of 'F' to create a 36.7-litre engine. This engine – the 'H', later renamed as the Buzzard – ran in mid-1928 and delivered 850hp.

Mitchell had been advised by Air Ministry

officials familiar with Rolls-Royce's development work that they may be receptive to the idea to build a racing engine based upon the 'H'. While Rowledge, Hives and the technical staff were indeed enthusiastic the board, once again, was divided, with Basil Johnson, the managing director, particularly opposed to involvement in any form of competition as he feared it could put at risk their reputation for reliability and excellence. The car division had long ago turned its back on any suggestion of racing for the same reason. It took the intervention of the Air Ministry and of Royce himself to force a decision in favour of the project and work then began on the 'Racing H', later renamed as the 'R'. In July 1928 Mitchell was provided with

BELOW The Rolls-Royce 'R' engine in 1929.

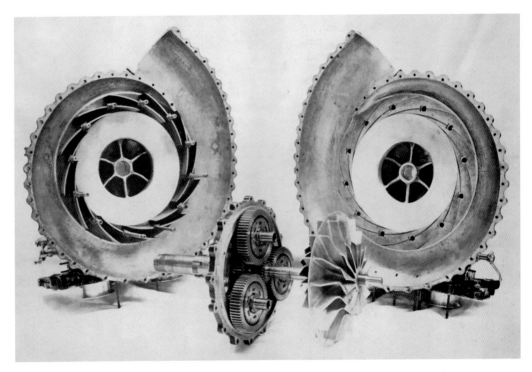

estimates of weight, power and silhouette by Hives's engineers sufficient for him to proceed with the design of the S6.

Design of the 'R' commenced as a straightforward racing development of the 'H' with which it would, at first, share many parts. The 'H' had benefited from the development programme for the 'F' and had addressed some of the shortcomings of this engine, notably the number and spacing of the cylinder block hold-down bolts to deal with water leaks. The team had set themselves a target power output of at least 1,500hp and based their calculations of fuel consumption and heat output around this so that Mitchell could design tanks and radiators accordingly. The key to this almost doubling in power, relative to the 'H', came down to three dominant factors: supercharging, higher revs and fuel formula. The 'H' and the 'F' before it had both incorporated moderate supercharging. For their development Rolls-Royce had employed James Ellor, a leading British expert in the field, who was previously at the RAE where he had worked with Rolls-Royce to achieve a substantial improvement in supercharger efficiency through careful attention to airflow. He would now lead the effort to design a special high-boost unit for the 'R'.

Mindful of the need to keep the frontal area of the engine to a minimum, a large-diameter supercharger impeller was not a viable option so a double-faced unit was designed fed by a forward-facing air intake positioned between the two cylinder banks. This intake led into a divergent duct that decelerated the air, thereby raising the pressure, and through four up-draught carburettors and a plenum chamber, before entering the twin eyes of the supercharger. The additional power produced by the engine as a result of the pressure rise achieved in the intake duct system was said to be roughly equivalent to the power required to drive the supercharger. The area of the intake throat was calculated so that the volume of air entering at a speed of 415mph – the speed of the slipstream behind the propeller at the expected top speed of the aircraft – exactly matched the requirements of the engine at maximum revs. In this way the intake added no drag. Ellor and Rolls-Royce patented the concept. The gearing of the supercharger drive was modified during the engine development programme to fine tune the boost pressure, which rose from 8psi in early runs to 12.25psi for the contest.

Rolls-Royce management authorised detailed design and fabrication in November 1928 and the Air Ministry issued a formal contract the following February. The prototype engine was run on the bench on 7 April 1929.

A small team, led by Ray Dorey, ran the test programme. Development of the 'R' was an iterative process: running an engine on the bench at progressively higher revs until failure, then redesigning the component that had failed and re-running the test. The first three engines, numbered R1, 3 and 5, were purely for bench development and not intended to be installed in aircraft, while numbers 7, 9, 11 and 15 (there was no 13 for superstitious reasons) would be for the two S6s, two allocated to each. In this way flight-testing was less likely to be subject to delay as the second engine would be readily available when the first was scheduled for servicing and would have benefited from any new upgrades.

The development engines were run in a test shed through which two 'F' engines and propellers provided an airflow – one into the supercharger air intake at the slipstream speed expected during the contest, and the other to clear exhaust fumes from the shed and for cooling. A single-cylinder test rig occupied a second shed while a third was for the development of the supercharger unit and carburettors in isolation. Early engine tests were run on neat benzole fuel and were plagued by excessive oil consumption and fuel pooling in the supercharger, yet within a month the engine was delivering more than the target power output of 1,500hp, albeit with a short life. The oil consumption problem was gradually solved by redesigning the baffles in the sump and by making revisions to the piston rings. By the end of the month the test engine was running on a petrol/benzole/TEL mixture. Connecting rod and bearing failures were addressed and by mid-July an engine was prepared for the one-hour acceptance run. This was achieved on a fuel of 11% petrol, 89% benzole and 2% TEL dope at a power output of 1,537hp at 2,750rpm. The engine was pushed to produce 1,614hp at 3,000rpm. Engine R7 was then cleared for flight and delivered to Supermarine for installation in the first S6, N247. Meanwhile, a one-hour test at full throttle, giving 1,568hp at 3,000rpm, was completed on 7 August on a revised fuel mixture of 22% petrol, 78% benzole and 2cc/gal TEL dope.

Rolls-Royce sent a small group to Calshot, led by Cyril Lovesey, to take responsibility for

LEFT The supercharger installed at the rear of the 'R' engine, the air intake duct to the right.

BELOW The supercharger design was refined in a special test rig before installation on the engine.

The highly tuned Napier Lion and Rolls-Royce 'R' racing engines both produced double the power of the production engines on which they were based and this required fuels of special composition. Standard aviation petrol was not acceptable for either.

During the First World War the supply of suitable fuels for the new generation of higher-powered engines had become increasingly problematic as resistance to pre-ignition, or 'knock', varied considerably between fuels provided by different suppliers. Early fuels had been graded based on an assessment of volatility, usually expressed by specific gravity, and while this had proven generally acceptable for the low-power engines and crude carburettors of the era, it was now becoming clear that the type and proportions of the various hydrocarbons in the fuel was of greater importance. Reaching agreement on a standard measure was not as straightforward as it first seemed and it took many years before the octane rating system was adopted. British fuels appeared to be significantly better for knock resistance than many US fuels. Recent analyses suggest that those refined from Rumanian or Far East crude oils, as was the case for most British supplies, had an octane rating of 70 to 75, while US fuels, except those derived from Californian crudes, were much lower at 45 to 55. This difference in knock resistance was due mainly to the higher aromatic, arene or 'ring', hydrocarbon content relative to the straight-chain paraffins, alkenes, in the British fuels. After the war products refined from coal-tar became readily available as an additional source for fuel, and these were predominantly composed of benzene and marketed as benzole. Benzole had high anti-knock qualities and became a common additive for aviation fuels.

Tetraethyl lead (TEL), an organic compound centred around a lead atom, was also introduced as a fuel additive in the mid-1920s as it was found to promoted anti-knock and had the additional benefit of protecting the engine valves.

The Napier Lion VIIA and B had a compression ratio of 10:1, which was very high for an aircraft engine. Early runs

experienced knock and other problems and adding too much benzole resulted in a build-up of soot, while adding too much TEL dope deposited lead on the plugs with consequent short-circuits. Napier called upon Francis Rodwell Banks, a fuel specialist with Peter Hooker Ltd, to aid them. The race fuel he recommended was a blend of 74.78% petrol, 25% benzole and 0.22% TEL dope which was provided by Pratts, the marketing division of Anglo-American Oil Co.

Early engine tests of the supercharged Rolls-Royce 'R' in 1929 were run on neat benzole fuel but this was soon changed to a mixture of petrol, benzole and TEL dope. Banks, now working for Anglo-American Oil Co., was employed as an adviser throughout the development phase. In 1931 new fuel formulas were devised by Banks to exploit the raised supercharger boost pressure and the cooler conditions in the cylinders that had resulted from the use of sodium-cooled exhaust valves. For the contest the mixture was 20% aviation petrol, 70% benzole, 10% methanol and 4cc/gal TEL. For the speed record run a special fuel was concocted composed of 30% benzole, 60% methanol, 10% acetone and 5cc/gal TEL.

In contrast to the carefully blended fuel formulas the lubricant used for both the Napier and Rolls-Royce engines was very simple – just basic castor oil. Various lubricants based on vegetable or mineral oils and blends of the two were in use at the time. Vegetable oils, mostly based on castor, did not break down at high temperatures (which was a problem with early mineral oils) and were less prone to dissolve in the presence of the fuel mixtures used in the racing engines. On the negative side, castor had a relatively high viscosity at low temperatures so it was necessary to preheat it before filling the tanks. Vegetable oils tend to polymerise at high temperatures and form a 'varnish' that coats the engine parts. This still had reasonable lubrication properties but was very difficult to remove as it was immune to most solvents, as anyone who has attempted to clean a deep-fat fryer will know.

the installation and adjustment of the engines in the S6. The first air-test was made on 10 August and there were no problems associated with the engine. As the date of the contest approached, Rolls-Royce had managed a bench run of 1hr 20min, giving 1,800hp at 2,850rpm on 22% petrol, 78% benzene and 6cc/gal TEL dope, and this was the state of development reached at the time of the contest flights. As already described, the power produced by the engines above the guaranteed 1,500hp, together with the additional heat that this generated, caused serious problems for Mitchell who had designed the cooling systems to deal with the lower output.

Despite their success, which the company were keen to celebrate in advertisements, Rolls-Royce were at pains to preserve the technical details of the engine, especially the supercharger installation, and no unretouched photographs or detailed information were released to the press.

A little development of the 'R' continued through 1930, partly funded by Lord Wakefield, of Castrol, who sponsored the construction of a boat for Major Segrave's attempt to take the world water speed record. His boat, *Miss England II,* was powered by two new 'R' engines, R17 and R19, where R17 was built to rotate in the opposite direction.

For the 1931 contest it was agreed that six new engines would be built, two for each S6B aircraft, with the aim to achieve 2,300hp by raising the boost from the supercharger and increasing engine revs. Bench testing and development was initiated using the 1929

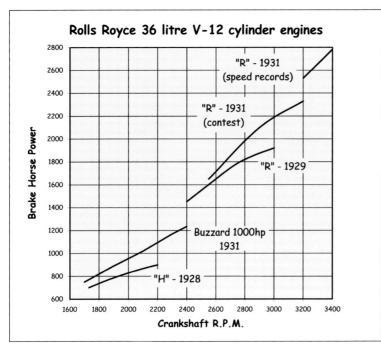

Rolls Royce 36 litre V-12 cylinder engines

Graph: Brake Horse Power (vertical axis, 600 to 2800) versus Crankshaft R.P.M. (horizontal axis, 1600 to 3400).

Curves labelled:
- "R" – 1931 (speed records)
- "R" – 1931 (contest)
- "R" – 1929
- Buzzard 1000hp 1931
- "H" – 1928

engines, primarily R3. The first runs took place in the closing days of February 1931 and an output of 2,300hp at 3,200rpm was soon achieved, but there were many issues to resolve regarding component strength, lubrication and heat dissipation before this could be sustained. The crankshaft bearings were in poor condition after a run and the 'knife and fork' big end bearings on the conrods were clearly unable to withstand the higher loads. With limited time and funds to undertake a full redesign it was decided that the only sensible option was to change to articulated conrods, although this would result in a slightly different stroke for the pistons on the master and slave sides.

Much of March was spent redesigning and fabricating parts. On 21 April the first run was made with a new crankcase, crankshaft and articulated conrods and two days later the engine ran for over a quarter of an hour at 1,900hp and 3,200rpm, but the bearings were badly scored and oil consumption was a worrying 50gal/hr. During a run the next day the main crankshaft bearing collapsed and the failure was repeated a week later, indicating that a redesign of both shaft and bearings was necessary. The precise reason for failure was not clear so the only option in the time remaining was to design a balanced crankshaft with a wider central bearing, which proved satisfactory but oil consumption had rocketed further to 76gal/hr with at least a third

of this lost through the crankcase breathers; the test shed walls dripped with castor oil. They were making progress but many compromises needed to be made.

In mid-May engine R7 was sent to Calshot, along with Lovesey and his team, to be installed in the refurbished S6A, N247, but it had to be returned to Derby to be stripped down and checked after seawater contaminated the fuel and was drawn into the engine. The first test-flight was eventually made on 2 June, but during a high-speed run it is thought that a combination of uneven engine revs and balance problems with the propeller were responsible for inducing flutter in the rudder that caused severe fatigue failure of the rear fuselage.

Engine testing continued throughout May but it was now plagued by a spate of exhaust valve spring failures, some causing the valves to drop into the cylinder, resulting in substantial damage. With new pistons, rings and a deeper crankcase with modified baffles the oil loss was finally brought under control, down to a more manageable 16gal/hr. At the end of June the company were able to plan to fit sodium-cooled exhaust valves, having acquired a subsidiary manufacturing licence from Bristol, who held the UK patent rights from Wilcox-Rich. These valves had hollow stems inside which molten sodium moved up and down to carry heat away from the valve crown and had been in use in some US engines since 1927.

Engine R15 was sent to Calshot for the second S6A, N248, where it made its first flight on 26 June, but these tests had to be curtailed after 10 minutes when the engine cut out. This happened twice more in the following days and was traced to fuel system sealant residue contaminating the fuel. The engine ran rough over 2,800rpm.

In early July R21, the first of the new-build engines destined for the S6B, was running at 2,292hp and was made ready to be sent to Supermarine. Meanwhile, the first set of sodium-cooled valves were completed for testing and had a profound effect on cooling; conventional valves had always reached red heat and caused problems with pre-ignition of the fuel. The new valves were a great success and with cooler conditions in the cylinder the fuel formula and mixture settings could be revised. At the end of the month an attempt was made to achieve the one-hour acceptance at 3,200rpm, but this failed just after half an hour when the crankshaft broke again. An investigation showed that this shaft had run for 71.5hrs in various tests, but when two more crankshaft failures occurred in the following days it prompted Rolls-Royce to establish a detailed log for every engine component. Each was then given an approved 'life' after which it would be replaced as a matter of routine. After a review of these and earlier crankshaft failures it was suspected that it was subject to some form of torsional resonance, but there was no time to investigate further. Another redesign was undertaken but this amounted to little more than additional localised strengthening. A full investigation into torsional resonance, on a theoretical basis, was eventually carried out by the RAE from 1933 and the results were published in 1935.

S6B, S1595, made its first flight on 29 July and the engine performed perfectly. Four more flights were made before the engine was removed and returned to Rolls-Royce for evaluation. R23 was sent to Supermarine for the second S6B in early August and around the same time R9, incorporating all the 1931 upgrades, completed the one-hour acceptance trial developing 2,350hp at 3,200rpm. Oil consumption was now down to 8gal/hr. On 9 September, a few days before the contest,

Rolls-Royce pushed R15 to the limit when it ran at 2,783hp at 3,400rpm with 20psi boost from the supercharger on a fuel mixture of 70% petrol, 30% benzole, and 5cc/gal TEL dope.

R25, R29 and R31 were designated as the contest engines and installed in S1596, S1595 and N248 respectively, while R27 was retained at Derby to be configured as a 'sprint' engine for a later attempt on the world absolute air speed record. The engine was fitted with fuel pumps giving increased flow and was rated at 2,530hp at 3,200rpm using 17.6psi boost from higher supercharger gearing and an enlarged air intake. It was the engine installed in S1595 when Flt Lt Stainforth established a new air speed record at 407.5mph.

No further flights were made with any of the three surviving S6 series aircraft after the speed record. In late 1932 the Engine Subcommittee of the ARC put forward a proposal to submit the five remaining 1931 'R' engines to test at the RAE. It was suggested that one should undertake the standard service type test running at a rating of 1,500hp at 2,750rpm and a boost pressure of 23.5psi. The other four would be run to destruction at various outputs between 1,500hp and 2,300hp to enable calibration of the RAE stress calculations for the individual components. However, it was pointed out that in such simple tests there would be considerable uncertainty as to the likelihood of obtaining

BELOW The ultimate Rolls-Royce 'R', engine R27, which was installed in the S6B for the speed record run that achieved 407.5mph.

useful results, especially if the engine was partially or completely wrecked in the process. Consequently this part of the programme was dropped. It appears unlikely that the type testing took place either, although some elements were probably included in Rolls-Royce's development of the Buzzard MS, an engine rated at 1,000hp that incorporated some 'R' technology and which was proposed for use in single-engine bombers and high-speed postal aircraft.

Propellers – Fairey-Reed

Curtiss-Reed metal propellers were a key factor in the success of Curtiss racers in the Schneider Trophy contest in 1923. When Fairey acquired the British licence rights to these propellers it was only natural that they would be called upon to provide them for Britain's Schneider Trophy racers for 1925.

Reed propellers were manufactured from a single flat light alloy bar that was tapered to the tips, machined to an aerofoil profile, and then twisted to the required pitch. The sharply twisted section adjacent to the flat hub was not always fully enclosed within the spinner. In the debate that followed the British failure at the 1925 contest, the Fairey-Reed propellers were singled out for criticism by GAC and provoked a spat between Fairey, GAC and Supermarine, who sided with GAC, played out in the correspondence pages of *Flight*. This was rekindled at a meeting of the Royal Aeronautical Society (RAeS) in early 1926 where GAC Chief Designer Henry Folland stated that there appeared to have been a loss of efficiency at high speed and suggested possible causes as torsion of the blade tips, straightening of the blades under centrifugal tension, or excessive tip speed. He quoted a tip speed of 1,120ft/sec for the Gloster III, which is just above the speed of sound, compared to about 950ft/sec for the Curtiss, which would suggest that his final point was probably correct. It was precisely this

RIGHT A Fairey-Reed metal racing propeller installed in the Gloster II. A similar propeller in the Gloster III came in for criticism.

observation that led to the decision to produce the Napier Lion in both ungeared and geared form for the 1927 racers.

While GAC elected to develop their own propellers for 1927, Supermarine decided to continue with Fairey-Reed types of a more sophisticated design. These were formed from forged ingots that were machined to shape, finished by hand and then given a final twisting to meet specific speed specifications.

Fairey were moving into unknown territory. Although they, and indeed Reed, were at first rather reluctant to acknowledge it, their 1925 propellers had left room for improvement. However, the amount of relevant propeller performance data available to guide them on the best way forward was very limited. Blade design had to be based largely on theoretical studies and on experiments carried out at small scale. The engine and aircraft designers presented them with figures for estimated engine power, revs and aircraft speed, and based on this Fairey's aerodynamics designer Pandia Ralli calculated the theoretical best blade diameter and pitch, made correction for tip speed and then a best estimate of the adjustments required to take into account the slipstream drag on the aircraft fuselage. From this he produced four different blade designs: a theoretical 'ideal' blade and three evolved from this with differing diameter, maximum chord and chord distribution. These four designs were built in two sets, one for the direct-drive engine and one for the geared example. During the flight-testing of the S5 aircraft it was not possible to carry out exhaustive tests on each propeller as time was limited, but a final design, close to the 'ideal' type, was produced for the contest. Analysis of the flight-test data accumulated through 1927 to 1931 showed that Fairey's 1927 propellers operated with a maximum efficiency of between 75% and 81% on the geared engine, and as low as 63% on the ungeared when the tip speed reached Mach 1.12.

The 1927 propellers provided a sound base upon which to design new types for installation in the S6 for the 1929 contest. The problems remained the same, but the propeller was now required to handle a substantial increase in engine power and higher aircraft top speed, although it was the initial acceleration to take-off speed that gave greatest cause for concern.

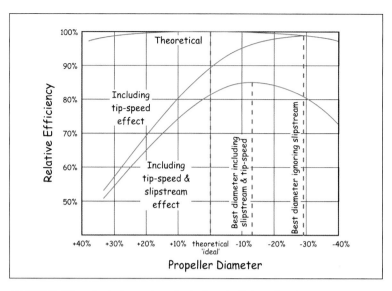

ABOVE Ralli's calculations when designing the Fairey-Reed propellers demonstrate how tip speed and slipstream effects impact the performance of propellers of various diameters.

BELOW This Fairey-Reed propeller of exaggerated chord distribution was one of several designs flight-tested.

ABOVE The propeller installed on the ungeared Napier Lion VIIA in the first Supermarine Napier S5, N219, for its first flight.

the torque reaction from the powerful geared engine would be severe. This had been known about in 1927, although the combined effects were shown to be manageable, but it would prove far more troublesome in 1929.

Fairey produced six alternative propellers, all of 9ft 6in diameter, but with differing pitch setting, maximum chord, maximum chord position and aerofoil camber. To provide the necessary strength and stability they were substantial castings each weighing around 200lb. Two of these designs were produced yet never installed and flown. The first tests of the S6, N247, confirmed the worst fears as the torque from the heavy propeller and powerful engine caused the port float to dig in and the aircraft to turn sharply. However, with the bulk of the fuel transferred to the starboard float tank it proved possible to gain sufficient control to accelerate to take-off speed, but it remained marginal. A propeller of slightly finer pitch improved matters but at the expense of a small reduction in top speed. The two S6s flew in the contest with different propeller types fitted; N248 proved slightly the faster of the two as the engine was allowed to run at higher revs. A third propeller was fitted to N247 for the speed record runs, but the speed reached was lower than had been hoped for and indicated that more research remained to be done.

In 1931 Fairey, in common with Rolls-Royce and Supermarine, had insufficient time to carry out much new design work. The amount of useful flight data obtained in 1929 on propeller performance was quite limited as the total number of flights made by the two S6s was less than 20 including the contest itself, and very little had been done in 1930. On the basis of what they had logged, and the estimated power, revs and speed expected from the developed 'R' engine, it seemed that the best option for 1931, with particular attention on improving take-off, would be to produce a propeller of reduced diameter, 8ft 6in appearing to be optimal. However, theory and practice proved to be poles apart and the S6B was completely uncontrollable on the water

The issue was threefold: first, that the high-pitch blades optimised for maximum speed were stalled at low air speed and generated a fraction of their potential thrust; second, the nose-up attitude of the aircraft right up to the moment of take-off meant that the propeller was operating at a pronounced angle to the airflow and hence generating asymmetric thrust from the ascending and descending blades; and, finally,

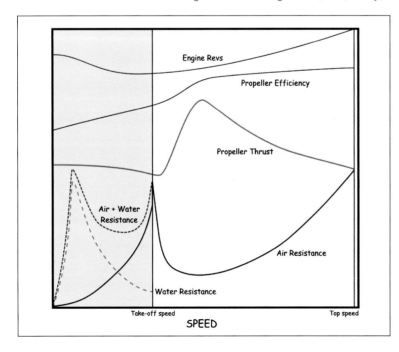

LEFT A schematic chart shows how peaks in air and water resistance combined with low thrust from the stalled propeller to create great difficulty in achieving initial acceleration and then take-off.

despite the improved floats and knowledge of the take-off techniques that had been refined with the S6 and S6A. It was very clear that the helical slipstream impacting on the fuselage, fin and rudder had a more detrimental effect on yaw and control surface effectiveness than had been assumed and so the propeller had to be abandoned. Fairey had six forged alloy blanks ready to be shaped into propellers, but two had already been cut down to be machined into the 8ft 6in design and hence had to be scrapped. A third was in an intermediate state and was reshaped for 8ft 10in, while the remaining three had the tips re-forged to 9ft 6in. While this work was under way one of the 1929 propellers that had been damaged at the tips was cut down to 9ft 1.5in and sent out to be used for practice flights. It proved to be particularly good and so was retained for the prime race aircraft, S1595, despite actually being a little marginal in strength for the new engine. S1596 had one of the 9ft 6in propellers installed and with this it established a new world air speed record, but more was expected from the aircraft when it had the special 'sprint' engine installed. For the next attempt with this engine it had been intended to use the 8ft 10in design, but this proved to be surprisingly poor so the decision was made to revert to one of the 9ft 6in designs and with this installed the aircraft established a new record of 407.5mph.

In order to understand why the problems had been so acute, three model Fairey propellers were constructed in laminated walnut to be added to the wind tunnel aircraft models and driven by an electric motor: one was based on the 1929 contest propeller, a second was of Fairey's preferred smaller-diameter design for 1931, and a third was for the design used for the contest. Producing accurate blade shapes proved troublesome and the first propeller was noticeably warped. The wind tunnel results, although limited, matched the observations at full scale with the aircraft.

An evaluation of all the flight data showed that the propellers used in 1931 all had efficiencies between 81% and 86% at top speed, which is very creditable and a notable improvement since 1927. Blades with wide bases tapering to pointed tips were generally found to be less efficient than those with broader chord mid-blade and more rounded tips.

LEFT The propeller on Supermarine Rolls-Royce S6A, N248.

BELOW Before and after: the forged Duralumin blank as delivered to Fairey and the finished propeller.

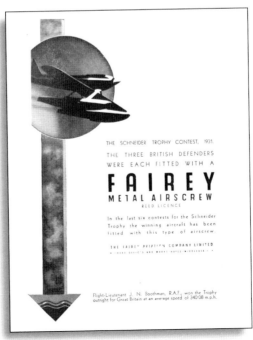

Chapter Four

Anatomy of the S6B and earlier Supermarine racing seaplanes

Supermarine's racing seaplanes were in a completely different league from the company's military flying boats alongside which they were built. Working on the small, sleek aircraft tested to the limit the skills of the workshop craftsmen.

OPPOSITE The first S6B, S1595, complete with wings and floats. The Rolls-Royce 'R' is in the process of being installed. In the background the fuselage of S1596 rests behind the tail surfaces for Southampton flying boats.

75

Chapter Four

Anatomy of the S6B and earlier Supermarine racing seaplanes

Supermarine's racing seaplanes were in a completely different league from the company's military flying boats alongside which they were built. Working on the small, sleek aircraft tested to the limit the skills of the workshop craftsmen.

OPPOSITE The first S6B, S1595, complete with wings and floats. The Rolls-Royce 'R' is in the process of being installed. In the background the fuselage of S1596 rests behind the tail surfaces for Southampton flying boats.

The main construction features of the S6B aircraft were essentially identical to those of the S6, with which it shared all but the floats, and honed from experience with the S5. All these aircraft were completely atypical of Supermarine's commercial products and contemporaneous project designs, and also quite different from the S4, despite this aircraft having been designed for the same purpose. The change in design style was not itself a direct result of the funding and research provided by the government, which it pre-dated by a few months, but Mitchell derived great benefit from their support.

Supermarine had been established with the express intent of becoming a specialised builder of flying boats. Founded as Pemberton-Billing Ltd by Noel Pemberton Billing in 1914 their first advertising material declared the company's aim to be '... the construction of a sea-worthy boat capable of attaining flight', but their first attempt, the Supermarine P.B.1, failed to fly. During the war the company forged a strong relationship with the Admiralty's aircraft design department and, among a variety of diverse tasks, built flying boats to their designs.

Relaunched as Supermarine Aviation Works in 1916 under their new managing director and former works manager Hubert Scott-Paine, the young company focussed increasingly on marine aircraft, an ambition restated in 1919 as 'a seaworthy hull that will fly'. The company works were staffed by woodworking craftsmen skilled in the best boatbuilding techniques, their premises were located on the banks of the river Itchen and they had no airfield. Not without some justification did they declare themselves as 'the most complete and up-to-date flying boat and seaplane works in the country'. The company's Schneider Trophy racers, Sea Lion, Sea Lion II and III, had all been flying boats and prior to its cancellation the Sea Urchin racer of 1924 would have been one too.

The Supermarine Napier S4

Mitchell's first step on the road to the S6B was something of a design and construction cul-de-sac, but worth describing in order to show how, for his racers, he was willing to discard ideas and start again in the

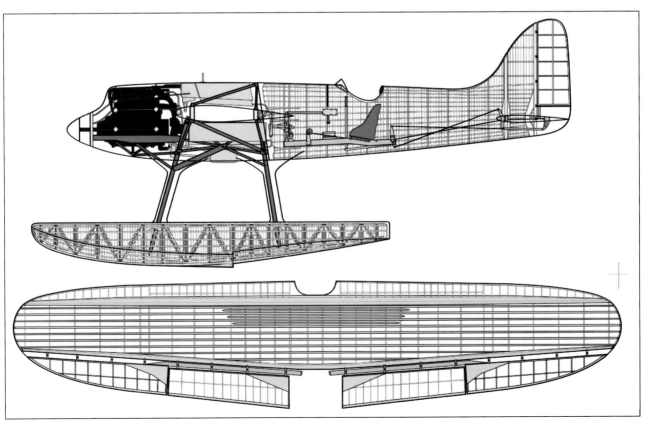

face of disappointment – something he was often more reluctant to do for the company's commercial products.

For Supermarine the decision to abandon racing flying boats in favour of a seaplane was not an easy one as this entailed embarking into unknown territory for Mitchell and his design team. They had no experience with monoplanes or with cantilever wings and negligible experience with seaplanes. The structural heart of the S4 was a framework built around two large 'A' frames fabricated from 2.158in 14G steel tubes, with the legs forming the pairs of fore and aft chassis struts that bolted to the floats. The two frames were connected and cross-braced at the top by multiple smaller tubular struts. The finished framework, referred to by the workers as 'the clotheshorse', enclosed the fuel tanks and incorporated the cantilever engine mounts for the Lion engine. Mitchell patented the structure, although it is hard to see why this was considered worthwhile. From the front of the cockpit rearwards the fuselage was a wooden semi-monocoque, built in a similar manner to Supermarine's flying boat hulls, and this bolted to the rear 'A' frame at two points and to the apex of a secondary pyramidal metal tubular structure attached to the top of the wing. The fin was formed as an integral part of the fuselage. For the wooden monoplane wing Mitchell selected the RAF30 symmetrical section aerofoil, which had a thickness-to-chord ratio of just 12.6%. It was built in one piece, tip to tip, on multiple spars with wood-ply skinning. The front and rear main spars bolted to brackets on the apexes of the 'A' frames and were braced laterally by two short vertical struts on either side from the 'A' frame legs. The wings incorporated large inboard flaps to reduce the landing speed, and these operated in conjunction with the ailerons, which drooped when the flaps were lowered. Each float was constructed around a longitudinal plywood bulkhead with large fretted triangular lightening holes and spruce stiffeners, to which transverse bulkhead frames were attached. The skinning followed the standard practice with the company's flying boats. Supermarine also drew plans for floats of the same shape to be fabricated in Duralumin and Oswald Short stated in a letter written in 1927 that

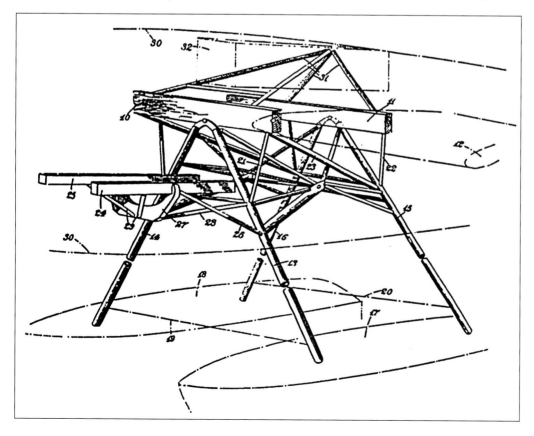

LEFT The patented metal-tube 'clotheshorse' frame of the S4.

RIGHT In one form of
the Lamblin radiator
the tubular vanes
projected below the
wing surface and
were aligned with the
slipstream. Although
superior to most
conventional radiators
they generated
significant drag.

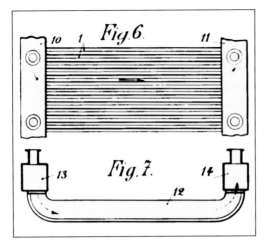

his company had built metal floats for the S4.
However, photographs of the aircraft show
neither panel laps nor rivets, strongly suggesting
that these were never fitted.

When the metal tubular framework was
covered by the numerous light sheet metal cowl
panels and fairings, the upper portion of the
'A' frames and all their bracing struts were fully
enclosed within. Mitchell followed the accepted
understanding of aerodynamics at this time to
achieve optimal streamlining. The fuselage was
of the shape generally referred to as 'airship'
or 'fish' with the position of maximum cross-

section area about one-third of the way down
the fuselage, roughly where the cockpit was
located. The cantilever wings sat at the mid-
fuselage position with the lateral engine cylinder
bank fairings merging into the leading edge.
As British companies had yet to master the
techniques to manufacture surface radiators,
long mastered by Curtiss and others, Mitchell
turned to the next best option, which was the
French underwing Lamblin tube-type that had
been developed for the Bernard-Ferbois V2 air
speed record aircraft the previous year. These
were partially recessed into the lower wing,
leaving just the multiple elongated flattened tube
radiator fins exposed.

The original intention was that the S4 would
have no external bracing, but during initial
engine runs the float chassis was seen to be
too prone to vibration so small lateral bracing
struts were added between each 'A' frame's
legs. It was an exceptionally well proportioned
aircraft but the view for the pilot was awful, most
especially so for Henry Biard, the company test
pilot, who was used to sitting in the nose of a
flying boat with an unimpeded view.

There does not appear to have been an official
investigation into the causes of the crash of the

S4 and the wreckage was most probably left in the USA. The two suggestions that the crash was caused either by wing flutter or high-speed stall are both plausible and in all probability there was an element of both involved. The 'A' frames and wing mounts were inherently flexible and the control to the flaps and ailerons involved a sequence of levers, ball joints and torque tubes that may well have been prone to excessive play. Whatever the cause, Mitchell learned the lesson and his subsequent seaplanes would share next to nothing from the S4 and employ a completely different form of construction.

The Supermarine Napier S5

The S5 concept design was a significant step away from the S4 and implies that Mitchell had undergone a fundamental rethink regarding the structure of his next racer. It is not clear whether the S5 was planned to be of metal construction from the start, but it is certainly likely as the company had recently committed to opening a metal-working department to build hulls for the Southampton flying boat and this was expected to be

fully functional by mid-1926. Final design and stress calculations for the S5 structure had to await the results of the wind tunnel evaluations, and by the time Supermarine had the necessary confirmation from the NPL and RAE the metalwork department was functional. Work was already under way on the experimental 48ft alloy hull for the Southampton and the diminutive 22ft S5 fuselage and 18ft 6in floats would be the next project to be tackled in the works.

The fuselage structure of the S5 comprised four longerons and two robust ventral intercostal beams, to which lightweight channel section transverse hoop frames were riveted. These frames were of modified elliptical shape, slightly flattened at the base and with 'shoulders' at the level of the upper longerons to accommodate the shape of the engine and its lateral cylinder banks. Somewhat inevitably, the story is told of Simmonds sitting with his back to a board while the outline for the fuselage cross section was drawn around him, and as he was not particularly large this accounts for the cramped size of the cockpit for some of the pilots. However, this is more than likely apocryphal, with similar stories cropping up for many other

BELOW The metal structure of the fuselage and floats, and wooden wings of the Supermarine Napier S5.

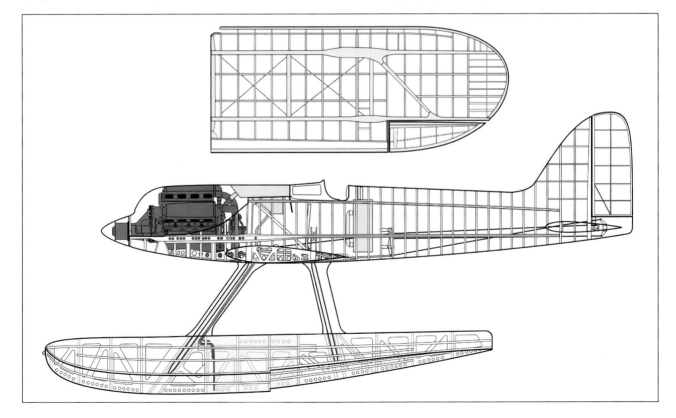

Stressed-skin metal construction for aircraft was by no means a new concept when Mitchell designed the S5, but as a technique it was still very much in its infancy. In Britain the pioneers in the fabrication of metal monocoques were Short Bros and Oswald Short made great efforts in the immediate post-war years to promote his business, convinced that the time was right to make a move from wood to metal construction. To demonstrate the potential of all-metal structures for aircraft, Short introduced the Swallow/Silver Streak single-seat biplane at the Olympia Aero Show in 1920 and took out a patent on the construction methods for the monocoque fuselage soon after. The Air Ministry purchased the aircraft for evaluation. With the exception of the tubular steel spars the aircraft was built entirely of Duralumin.

Duralumin, an alloy of aluminium containing 4% copper, 0.5% magnesium and 0.5% manganese, was developed at Dürener Metallwerke in Germany in 1903. After heat treatment and age hardening it is an alloy that can be wrought, drawn, rolled and worked to shape, and was soon adopted by the German aviation industry, especially for dirigibles, as it combined the low density of aluminium with tensile strength and durability more comparable to steel. In Britain a licence to manufacture was purchased by James Booth and Co. (1915) Ltd, a division of Vickers until 1928. In the early years the alloy's use in Britain remained rather limited as its resistance to corrosion and fatigue had yet to be assessed and there were no official standards. The depressed state of the economy in the post-war years was not perhaps the best time to introduce new technology but Shorts were persistent and built several types, including the diminutive S.1 Stelite/Cockle flying boat and the S.2 experimental hull for a Felixstowe F.5 flying boat, both in 1923. Air Ministry tests on the Swallow and on Duralumin samples soon established the fatigue characteristics of the metal, while Shorts' immersion tests of samples in seawater had laid to rest many of the concerns surrounding corrosion. Shorts had certainly proven themselves as the premier builders of monocoque hulls,

floats and fuselages in metal and the Air Ministry was on the verge of specifying metal hulls for all future flying boats. The other aircraft companies had to respond and Supermarine were at the forefront.

Supermarine had designed a single-engine all-metal flying boat in 1918 but at that time had neither the facilities nor expertise to build such an aircraft. However, towards the end of 1925 the company recruited Arthur Black, a metallurgist working for Brown Firth Research Laboratories, to head and set up a metalworking department and had a contract from the Air Ministry to produce an experimental metal hull for the Southampton flying boat. It appears that the new department was able to work and treat standard Duralumin sheets measuring 2ft x 6ft, which were available in various thicknesses, or gauges.

Gauge	Thickness in inches
14	0.080
16	0.064
18	0.048
20	0.036
22	0.028
24	0.022

The hull for the Southampton II proved to be an immediate success and led to multiple orders, Supermarine effectively leap-frogging Shorts for commercial success with metal-hulled flying boats. By the end of the 1920s Supermarine's woodworking department was reduced to a minor part of the workforce.

Forged Duralumin ingots were supplied to Fairey by James Booth for fabrication of their racing propellers and are believed to have been the largest such forgings produced at the time.

High tensile steel produced by Thomas Firth & John Brown Ltd was used for the float strut tubes and the bracing wires, and Firth Staybrite steel was used for the fuel tanks, fin and oil coolers. The company also supplied special steel alloys for the conrods, camshafts, gears and many other components in the 'R' engine. The crankshafts were forged from steel alloys by the English Steel Corporation.

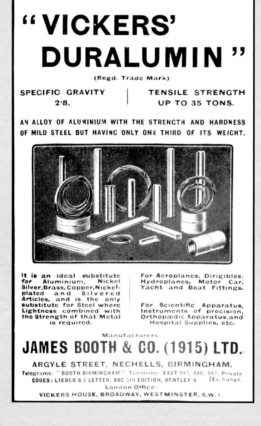

aircraft over the years. The actual dimensions for the S5 were dictated primarily by the size of the engine and Mitchell's desire to fit the cockpit within its silhouette.

Suitably thickened and strengthened, the lower longerons extended to the nose and formed cantilevered engine bearers, the resultant scoop-shape of the lower nose referred to as a 'coal scuttle' by Mitchell. There was a reinforced firewall bulkhead to the rear of the engine bay and stouter partial frames for the key stress points where the rear wing spars and float struts attached. The front spar and float struts attached to the reinforced bulkhead. The fuselage was then plated with Duralumin sheeting, doubled or tripled at high stress points. The fin was an integral part of the fuselage and the tailplane spar was built into the structure.

The first fuselage was subjected to proof load testing: 4,640lb on the engine bearers, 550lb on the tail, and subsequently a side-load on the fin of 385lb. Deflection was not excessive, the elastic limit was not exceeded and there was no damage.

For the floats, the framework emulated that used for the S4's wooden floats. A longitudinal Duralumin keel frame, with cut-outs to reduce weight, was reinforced with angle pieces. Transverse frames and watertight bulkheads were then attached and linked by longitudinal stringers of 'L' section. The whole frame was then skinned with Duralumin plates, with the exception of the central portion of the starboard float where the skinning and bulkheads were of tinned steel to form an integral 55gal fuel tank. This was a late revision to the initial design where the fuel tanks were intended to be separate cylindrical units enclosed within each float. The steel tube float chassis struts were secured between reinforced bulkheads and were rigged asymmetrically with the starboard float 6in further out from the centreline than the port which, along with the fuel, was to provide an offset load to help counter the torque from the engine, especially for take-off. This received adverse comment at the time as some felt that the offset load in the air would require an unwanted application of aileron to fly level, but this appears to have been largely unfounded.

BELOW The offset starboard float of S5, N219, is very apparent in this head-on view.

ABOVE Napier engineers work on the engine of S5, N221, prior to an attempt on the world air speed record in 1928.

The wings, in contrast to the fuselage and floats, were of wooden construction, because the company was not yet sufficiently experienced to attempt construction in metal. The primary structure comprised two built-up box spars and a robust diagonal torsion member to stabilise the aileron hinges. Light ribs were attached flush with the spars and the whole was then skinned with ⅛in 3-ply wood. Wing surface radiators were screwed to the upper and lower surfaces. These were fabricated from copper sheets in sections 8in wide – the outer surface was flat, while the inner was corrugated and was sweated together to form chord-wise channel ways. The completed 60in x 8in units were sweated and riveted together with copper input and output pipes, soldered in place at the nose and tail to form the final radiator, which extended over the full chord of the wing, except at the tips and ailerons.

A cylindrical oil tank was placed vertically in the fuselage behind the pilot. Corrugated coolers were fitted on either side of the fuselage, with one taking hot oil from the engine to the tank and the other returning it. Each cooler had three corrugation channels and was about 6ft long. After early flight-testing it was found that cooling was marginal so replacement coolers, 11ft long and with four corrugations,

were fabricated to replace them. A number of cooling scoops and vents were added to the nose of the fuselage and engine fairing pieces.

The Supermarine Napier S5 proved to be a most successful aircraft so it might be expected that Mitchell would have chosen to simply enlarge and strengthen the S5 structure to meet the requirements for the S6, but that was not the way he worked. As a consequence, although there is a strong family resemblance in the shape of the two, the S6 was a very different aircraft.

The Supermarine Rolls-Royce S6 and S6B

As Mitchell had tailored the fuselage of the S5 to fit the Lion engine like a glove it had been extremely narrow around the cockpit, to the extent that access had proven to be a problem for some larger pilots who found their shoulders were jammed against the sides. The sitting position was also cramped in the short cockpit with the pilot's knees at chest height. Although Mitchell intended to continue with the same broad design philosophy for the S6, the larger dimensions of the Rolls-Royce 'R' alleviated many of these problems and the fuselage could be of simple elliptical section throughout.

LEFT The first Supermarine Rolls-Royce S6 on display at Calshot.

The fuselages for the two S6 aircraft were constructed in adjacent jigs. A framework of stout beams enclosed and supported these jigs and within each a series of trestles, secured to the framework, supported a longitudinal plank mounted on its edge and shaped to conform to the lower contours of the fuselage. A similar plank for the upper contours was suspended from the overhead framework beams by sloping trusses.

BELOW Two wooden jigs support the fuselage frames prior to plating. S6B, S1596, is in the foreground with S1595 behind.

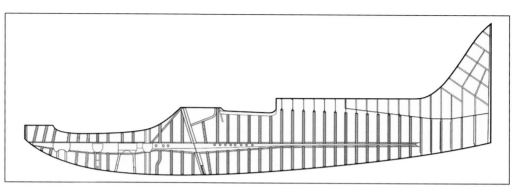

RIGHT The internal structure of the S6 fuselage showing the single longeron, the lightweight hoop frames, the robust engine bay bulkhead and engine supports.

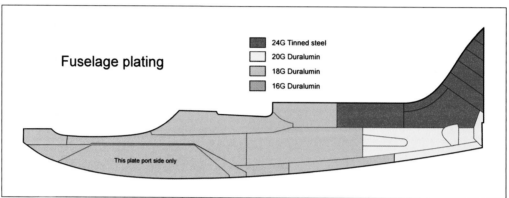

Fuselage plating

- 24G Tinned steel
- 20G Duralumin
- 18G Duralumin
- 16G Duralumin

This plate port side only

RIGHT The fuselage was plated with Duralumin sheets of various thicknesses, depending on the local load. Plates were doubled or tripled in areas subject to high stress.

The stations for the 46 transverse formers and bulkheads, generally spaced at 6 to 7in, were then marked on the jig planks and the component parts aligned and held in place with clamps. The majority of the formers were of simple flanged channel section rolled from 18G Duralumin, but frames of thicker gauge were fabricated to take the front wing stub spar and front float strut attachment brackets, and for strengthening around the engine bay. A sloping double-faced bulkhead, lined with asbestos, separated the engine bay from the cockpit and served to hold the rear stub spar and lugs for the float struts. The bulkhead was perforated for the passage of the engine controls, rudder and aileron lines and piping. Only two longitudinal members were employed in the fuselage construction and these extended from the nose back to a few frames short of the rudder post. The nose sections were reinforced to form the engine bearers and were built up from 14G Duralumin; rearwards, they tapered to a simple flanged channel section of

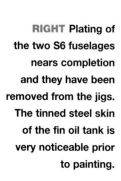

RIGHT Plating of the two S6 fuselages nears completion and they have been removed from the jigs. The tinned steel skin of the fin oil tank is very noticeable prior to painting.

LEFT An S6B fuselage, partially painted with chromate primer, has been drilled ready for installation of the side oil coolers. In the background is S5, N220, undergoing overhaul.

16 and 18G Duralumin. The engine bay was further strengthened by short intercostal box sections on either side.

In 1931 the first S6A, N247, experienced severe flutter of the rudder and elevators while travelling at top speed, induced by resonance (it was believed) from an unbalanced propeller and uneven engine revs. A similar phenomenon had occurred, but not destructively, during an early flight of the S5. The plating in the tail just ahead of and below the leading edge of the tailplane on the port side of the fuselage buckled and cracked, which required urgent investigation by the RAE. The rivets were drilled out and the damaged plating removed and sent to the RAE where the cracks were examined under the microscope. The Duralumin showed no signs of corrosion and samples subjected to tensile and bend tests showed that they conformed to the industry's official requirements of BS Specification 3L.3. Although the crack surfaces did not show the characteristic signs

BELOW The corrugated oil cooler has now been screwed to the S6B fuselage. In the background is a wooden mock-up for an unbuilt flying boat project.

ABOVE Work continues on S1595 to install the engine. The supercharger intake cover has a vertical spike as an indicator that can be seen from the cockpit, and the splines on the propeller shaft are protected.

RIGHT The dome-head rivets used on the tinned steel skin for the fin oil tank are very apparent on S6A, N248.

of fatigue, it was concluded that they had to have been formed by concentrations of stress in excess of the fatigue range of the metal. The frequency of the flutter had been about 5Hz and had persisted from the top speed of the aircraft, around 350mph, until it had dropped back to below 200mph after the engine had been shut down. N247 was repaired with local strengthening, and this was also applied to N248 and the two new S6Bs.

The rudder and elevators were metal framed with 22G skins. On the trailing edge of the S6B's elevators a narrow tapering strip acted as a spoiler and could be easily bent by hand tools. On the S6B's rudder, and on all tail surfaces of the S6As, a short tab of Duralumin was riveted to the trailing edges and fulfilled

OPPOSITE The engine bay of the S6. The engine was bolted down firmly at the front and via rubber bushes at the rear to allow for expansion.

(C. Michell)

Supermarine S6B cutaway. *(Mike Badrocke)*

1 Mooring point
2 Starboard float
3 Float double-skinned surface radiator panel
4 Spinner
5 Propeller attachment
6 Splined propeller shaft
7 Fairey-Reed two-bladed fixed-pitch propeller
8 Propeller reduction gearbox
9 Cooling air scoop
10 Cylinder head fairings
11 External oil radiator piping, port and starboard
12 Float access panel
13 Float strut attachment joint
14 Engine bearer
15 Main engine mounting
16 Cylinder head exhaust ports (no exhaust pipes)
17 Fairey cylinder head rocker box covers
18 Rolls-Royce 'R' V12 inline racing engine
19 Starboard wing ventral flying wires
20 Upper surface lifting wires
21 Starboard wing surface water radiator panel
22 Wing tip fairing
23 Starboard aileron
24 Aileron mass balance weight
25 Aileron hinge control lever
26 Aileron cables
27 Fixed portion of trailing edge
28 Cylinder head aft fairing
29 Cooling air louvres
30 Engine air intake
31 Engine throttle and ignition controls
32 Supercharger
33 Fuselage main longeron
34 Engine supercharger intake ducting
35 Cooling water return pipes from engine
36 Water filler cap
37 Water system header tank
38 Engine compartment sloping bulkhead
39 Fuel system header tank
40 Rudder pedals
41 Control column
42 Engine throttle lever
43 Instrument panel
44 Ignition switches
45 Water system overboard vent pipe, starboard side
46 Forward hinged cockpit canopy cover
47 Safety harness
48 Pilot's seat
49 Headrest
50 Dorsal head fairing frames
51 Fin and root fillet integral oil tank
52 Fin root fillet construction
53 Starboard tailplane
54 Starboard elevator
55 Tailfin construction
56 Oil filler cap
57 Sternpost
58 Fabric-covered rudder construction
59 Rudder mass balance weight
60 Fixed tab
61 Rudder and elevator hinge control levers
62 Elevator fixed tab
63 Port elevator construction
64 Tailplane construction
65 Oil filter
66 Access plate
67 Port oil radiator tubing, feeding to fin oil tank
68 Ventral oil return pipes to engine
69 Tailplane control cables
70 Closely pitched fuselage frame construction
71 Control cable lever assembly
72 Starboard float tail fairing
73 Wing root fillet
74 Water feed pipes to wing radiators, upper and lower surfaces
75 Fixed portion of trailing edge
76 Port float rear buoyancy compartment
77 Float double-skin water radiator panel
78 Rear mooring point
79 Float tail fairing
80 Aileron mass balance weight
81 Port aileron

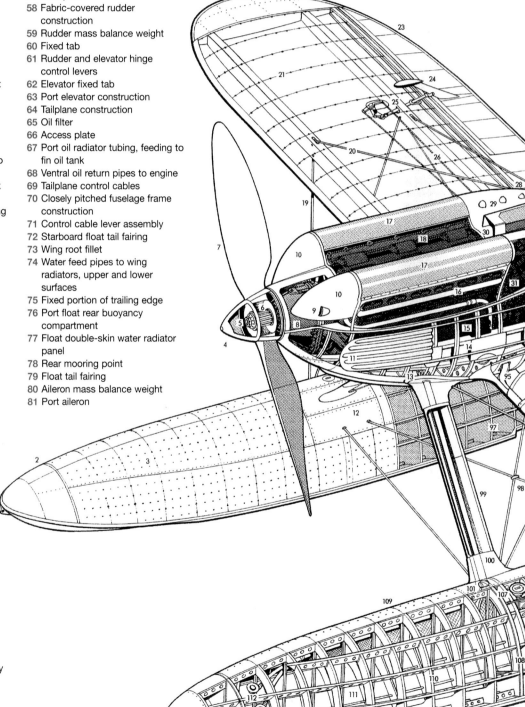

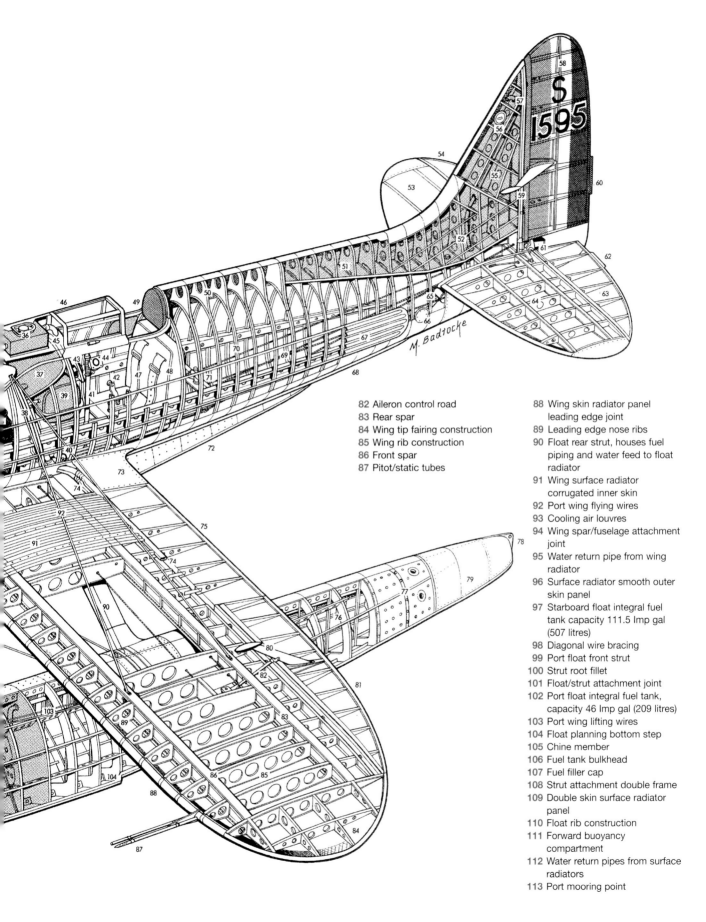

82 Aileron control road
83 Rear spar
84 Wing tip fairing construction
85 Wing rib construction
86 Front spar
87 Pitot/static tubes

88 Wing skin radiator panel leading edge joint
89 Leading edge nose ribs
90 Float rear strut, houses fuel piping and water feed to float radiator
91 Wing surface radiator corrugated inner skin
92 Port wing flying wires
93 Cooling air louvres
94 Wing spar/fuselage attachment joint
95 Water return pipe from wing radiator
96 Surface radiator smooth outer skin panel
97 Starboard float integral fuel tank capacity 111.5 Imp gal (507 litres)
98 Diagonal wire bracing
99 Port float front strut
100 Strut root fillet
101 Float/strut attachment joint
102 Port float integral fuel tank, capacity 46 Imp gal (209 litres)
103 Port wing lifting wires
104 Float planning bottom step
105 Chine member
106 Fuel tank bulkhead
107 Fuel filler cap
108 Strut attachment double frame
109 Double skin surface radiator panel
110 Float rib construction
111 Forward buoyancy compartment
112 Water return pipes from surface radiators
113 Port mooring point

A rear view of the S6A highlights the narrow fuselage behind the Rolls-Royce 'R' engine. Note the skinning of the tailplane, the elevator trim tabs and rudder mass balances.

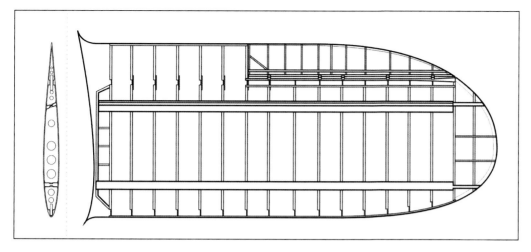

the same purpose. After N247's severe rudder flutter it was decided to add mass balances and to change the covering to fabric to reduce weight behind the hinge. The elevators were not treated the same way as it was felt that their flutter was secondary and had been induced by the rudder.

The wings were of all-metal construction on two spars rolled from 14G Duralumin strips. Both spars were of box section and built of two channel section webs with outward turned flanges to which flat strip flanges were riveted top and bottom. Each web had a single span-wise inward corrugation for added strength, except at the points where the external bracing wires attached, which remained flat, and were

ABOVE A section through the S6 wing shows the twin spars, a rib with punched lightening holes and, in red, the wing radiator inlet and outlet channels and narrow water passage between the skins.

BELOW A mass balance attached to the aileron activation lever as a precaution against flutter.

doubled or tripled at stress points. The webs of the rear spar were canted to match the slope angle of the rear engine bay bulkhead and the stub spar to which they connected. The ribs, spaced at 9.5in centres, were fabricated from 16G Duralumin in three sections – nose, centre and tail – in order to lie flush with the spars. The nose and tail ribs were notched to allow the passage of the wing radiator inlet and outlet feeder channels, and on the tail ribs this required strengthening plates to be riveted to the diaphragms. Each rib diaphragm had punched and flanged lightening holes and angled strip flanges riveted around the periphery, which had drilled holes for the attachment of the wing skins. The ribs were riveted to the spars using angle pieces. It was a complicated form of construction requiring many small components in the assembly. The

metal wing skins were also the surface radiators for the water cooling system.

The ailerons were metal framed and covered with 22G Duralumin skins. When it was found necessary to add mass balances to the rudder to guard against the occurrence of flutter, the same were added to the ailerons as a precaution. There had been some instances of incipient flutter experienced with the S5 when their hinges became worn or the tension in the control cables dropped.

The floats for the S6 were built in exactly the same manner as those on the S5. The longitudinal bulkhead was fabricated from 18G Duralumin and heavily perforated with rounded triangular lightening holes and strengthened with diagonal angle strips riveted in place. Transverse frames, spaced between 15in and 18in apart, were riveted to the bulkhead via angled pieces and were notched at their outer edge for the attachment of rolled, flanged and perforated 18G and 20G intercostal stringers. The skinning on the bottom surfaces was 16G and 18G, and 20G on the upper. Flush riveting was used throughout. The central portion of the float between the chassis struts formed an integral fuel tank, larger in the starboard float, and this portion was sealed by 22G bulkheads fore and aft and skinned with 24G plates, all in tinned steel. The struts were built into the float structure, each fixed between robust frames. They were 2in-diameter steel tubes, 17G for the rear and 8G for the front, which had to carry part of the static load of the engine. Where the struts entered the float they passed through nested tongued sleeves for strength. A socket at the top end of each strut attached to a lug on the fuselage with a single bolt.

During early testing of the S6 in 1929 it was found that the floats were rather marginal in

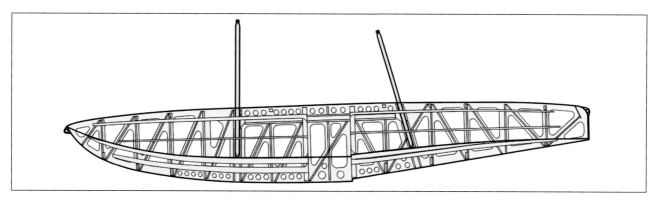

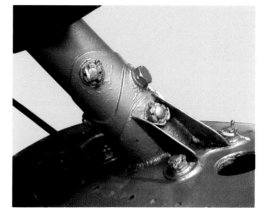

ABOVE The
internal structure of
an S6 float.

FAR LEFT AND
LEFT Nested-tube
strengthening where
a chassis strut exits
the float and the single
bolt attachment to the
fuselage wing stub
frame. Also shown
are the two bolts that
attached the wing spar
to the stub frame.

reserve buoyancy and Mitchell was concerned that their noses, rather low to improve aerodynamic drag, could dive below the water surface, especially on the port side, which was subjected to torque loading equivalent to an additional 500lb during acceleration. Consequently he had spare floats constructed, which had a lengthened and raised nose, although strangely these were only used on the starboard side. An attempt was made to solve the problem of the float sterns submerging during the acceleration phase on the water by attaching a device that added buoyancy and was fitted with small hydrofoils. They were tried just once on N248 and induced porpoising, so were discarded. No photographs or drawings of these devices have been found.

For 1931 the floats were the only part of the aircraft that were redesigned. For the upgraded S6s, designated as S6A, the extent of the redesign was relatively small and was aimed mainly at improving reserve buoyancy. The mid-sections remained the same as for the S6 floats, but the nose and tail were both lengthened and re-profiled. Port and starboard floats were of identical shape and length.

For the new-build S6Bs a completely revised and lengthened float was designed with a modified planing bottom profile, and

BELOW The
internal structure of
an S6B float.

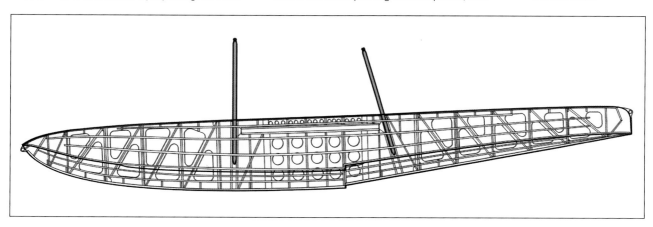

the float sides extended down by about 1in below the chines of the forebody to improve performance on the water. The internal framework construction remained substantially as before, with integral fuel tanks of 48gal in the port float and 110gal in the starboard, but the radiators were designed to function as the outer skinning, in the same manner as they did for the wings. Each radiator was attached by bolts and screws to the float frames and intercostals.

The simplicity of the aircraft's structure facilitated erection and rigging. The front and rear wing spars were attached to the fuselage stub spars by two bolts each, and the float struts hinged to the fuselage lugs with single bolts. The bracing wires were then attached and tensioned to maintain the correct alignment. The primary bracing comprised twin lift wires from the wing spars to the robust float frames at the base of the struts, lateral wires between the floats from the same frames, and twin wires from the apex of the rear engine bay bulkhead to the spars. The rear spar bracing wires lay in the same plane as the engine bay bulkhead, the rear spars and rear float struts, while the front spar bracing wires were also coplanar, thereby minimising torsion or unbalanced stresses in the system. Diagonal stabilising wires were also added between the fore and aft float struts, between the lift wire pairs, and between the inter-float lateral wires. The pair between the lift wires were omitted for the speed record runs.

The second S6B, S1596, turned out to be nearly 2% heavier than the first, S1595, and the reasons for this were never fully resolved.

Pilot's controls and instruments

The cockpit of the S6 was stark and minimalist but a definite improvement on the S5's cramped interior. Behind the engine bay bulkhead two lightweight longitudinal floor girders and a cross-piece formed the base for the cockpit, supporting the mounting for the control stick torque shaft and the rudder pedal pivot. The pilot's seat cushion was bolted to the rear while the seat back was separate and bolted to a frame attached to the fuselage sides at the rear of the cockpit. A three-point shoulder harness was incorporated. A small cushioned pad was attached to the starboard top cockpit edge to act as head protection during the high-g left turns experienced during the contests. The canopy comprised a light frame with three flat glass panels, one on the top and two side panels, which angled inwards slightly to the front. It hinged forward on its top front edge and was secured by sprung bolts on either side that were unlatched by a light

cable running forward and through a ring on the instrument panel. It was therefore within easy reach of the pilot should he need to make a quick exit. The canopy was also fitted with two small external scoops to provide cooling air to the pilot, which he could direct through a short length of hose. As in the S5 some pilots found that the best method to enter was to step in facing sideways, lower into position until shoulders were below the cockpit edge and then turn to face the front.

All the flight controls were activated by simple cranks and cables as in the S5. The universal joint for the control stick was attached to a torque shaft, which extended forward through the bulkhead. The aileron cable activation lever was fitted on the forward end and the cables ran out through the wings just ahead of the rear spar. The horizontal aileron control lever was enclosed within the wing and drove the aileron control rod, which protruded through the top of the wing surface. This lever on the aileron was later utilised as the mounting for the anti-flutter mass balance. All the internal

LEFT The cockpit canopy hinged forward and was secured by a sprung bolt on either side, which are not engaged in this photograph. (C. Michell)

RIGHT The lower part of the S6B cockpit showing the rudder pedals, control stick, engine throttle and mixture lever, fuel header tank and lower instrument panel. *(C. Michell)*

FAR RIGHT The rudder and elevator rocker levers and cables located behind the pilot's seat. *(C. Michell)*

BELOW The throttle, with red knob, and engine mixture control below. The ignition master switch is half hidden behind the throttle. *(C. Michell)*

levers and cable turnbuckles could be reached through access ports incorporated in the wing surface radiators. The rudder pedals moved fore and aft in guide tubes with a connecting pivot bar ahead of the bulkhead, while the control cables were attached to the sides of the rudder pedals and threaded through simple sleeve guides on the cockpit sides, passing around the pilot and connecting to the tips of a rocker lever mounted on a frame fixed to the fuselage sides behind his seat. From connectors inboard on this rocker, cables ran to the rudder activation

lever, which was fully enclosed within the fuselage tail and tailplane. The control stick had a ball-and-socket joint at its base that drove a connecting rod running under the pilot's seat to the tip of a rocker lever on the same frame as the rudder lever. Cables then ran to the elevator control lever in the tail. The controls at the tail could be accessed by removing the fuselage tail fairing below the rudder and through access panels in the rear fuselage. In 1929 the control column was fitted with an adjustable bungee, pulling forward, to alleviate some of the load at high speed. In 1931 a better solution was found by fitting thin alloy strips along the trailing edge of the elevators and bending these manually as required to adjust trim.

There were two engine controls to the pilot's left: the throttle and fuel mixture control. Prior to flight, the required fuel mixture was set by the Rolls-Royce engineer and locked-off.

The flight instruments were split between two panels, a standard panel at the front of the cockpit and a secondary panel on the floor ahead of the control stick. The aircraft was always constrained by the limitations of the cooling systems and the engine could be run at full throttle only briefly, therefore the pilot had to keep a close eye on the water temperature gauge and manage the engine revs accordingly. Air speed was measured via a pitot tube on

the port wing tip, but monitoring the air speed indicator was of little relevance during flight except when on approach and landing. For the contest the oil and boost gauges were disconnected at the engine and blanked off.

Fuel system

Fuel for the S6B was held in two tanks constructed as integral parts of the floats, with the tank in the starboard float holding 110gal and that in the port 48gal. Bulkhead

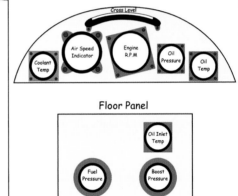

LEFT Arrangement of gauges.

BELOW S6B fuel system.

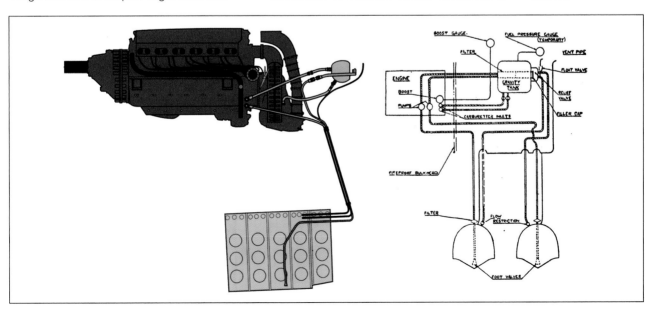

RIGHT Anti-slosh baffle plate within the S6B float fuel tank. The float radiator panels are separated from the tank by a small air gap.

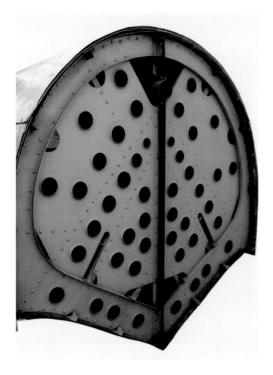

The valves maintained a pressure of around 6lb/in^2 in the header tank. Overflow pipes to the float tanks were vented in order to reduce the possibility of more fuel returning to one tank than the other. During high-g turns the acceleration force was sufficient to prevent the suction pumps drawing fuel from the floats, hence the header tank had to be of sufficient size to hold enough fuel to feed the engine during the turn and was equipped with external valves to admit air to prevent a partial vacuum forming.

Ensuring an even fuel overflow from the header back to the float tanks was a particular headache for the Supermarine technicians as it had an adverse effect on the lateral trim of the aircraft. A test rig was constructed to evaluate various restricting olives and air vents in the fuel lines. A solution was found and installed on the aircraft that gave satisfactory results, but changes to the gearing of the fuel pumps for the speed record runs raised the pressure in the system and upset the balance, which required further changes to the relief valves and overflow restrictions.

The S6B's engine consumed fuel at a rate of around 3gal/min under contest racing conditions and this, it was said, was roughly equivalent to the speed at which a man could pour fuel from a standard 2gal fuel can. The fuel pumps delivered fuel to the header tank at around 8.5 gal/min.

frames and skinning was in 24G tinned steel. A 3.5gal header tank was located in the cockpit behind and below the main instrument panel and this supplied the carburettors. The fuel pumps driven by the engine drew fuel from the float tanks and fed into the header tank, with the surplus flowing through special relief valves and overflow pipes back down to the floats.

BELOW S6B oil system.

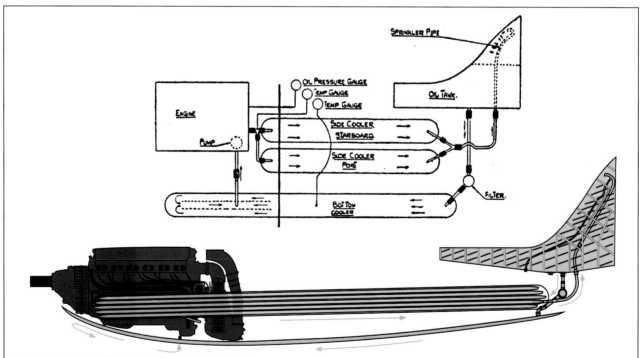

Oil system

The total capacity of the S6B oil system with its tank and fuselage corrugated coolers was 23.75gal and circulated at a rate of 7.2gal/min. During the duration of the contest – 54 minutes in total, of which 47 minutes was in the air – half of this oil was consumed. Oil left the engine at 100°C or slightly above and dropped by between 30° and 40°C across the cooling system. The fin, an integral part of the fuselage structure, was sealed and skinned with tinned steel to form the oil tank and part of the cooling system. For the S6B the capacity of the tank had been increased by extending it further forward into the fuselage dorsal spine, and the cooling efficiency was enhanced by sweating a series of sloping gutters to the inner surface of the skins to keep the oil in contact with the outer cooling surface for as long as possible. The twin side oil coolers were built of tinned steel. They were 18ft long, 8in wide and had five longitudinal corrugations 1¼in wide and ⅜in high that formed the channels for the oil. The cooler was bolted to the fuselage, with a small air gap, at a slight angle to the aircraft thrust line. For 1931 their cooling capacity was increased by as much as 40% by sweating small copper foil tongues within the corrugations to channel heat to the surface, and these were staggered to impede the flow as little as possible. The ventral cooler was about 19ft long and ran from nose to tail of the fuselage. It, too, was corrugated, with the central corrugation of roughly triangular section and about 1½in high. The outer corrugations mirrored those on the side coolers, and were paired on either side at nose and tail but merged into single corrugations each side where the coolers passed between the float struts and under the wing. This cooler was riveted in place and contributed to the structural strength of the fuselage. The total cooling area of the whole system was 67.8sq ft compared to just 11sq ft on the S5.

Oil was pumped from the engine to input pipes at the nose of each side cooler where it spread to enter all the corrugation channels. Merging again to the outlet pipes at the rear it then flowed to the top of the fin tank via a single perforated pipe that sprayed the oil on to the

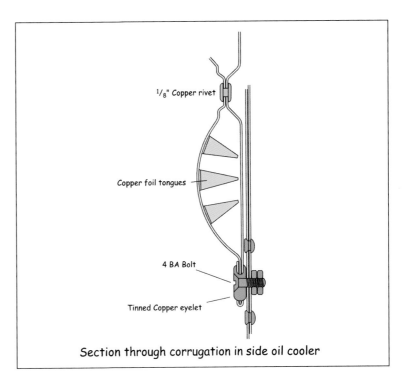

Section through corrugation in side oil cooler

tank skins, where it ran down to the reservoir. Oil exited through the base of the tank and passed through the oil filter before entering the rear of the ventral cooler. The outlet pipe was located under the engine and drew oil from the central corrugation only. Oil from the outer corrugations continued forward to the nose where it merged and then flowed rearwards down the central corrugation to the outlet.

Water system

The water cooling system on the various S6 aircraft underwent a process of continuous modification and extension as the power of the 'R' engine grew, with a consequent increase in the quantity of heat that needed to be dissipated. After the success of the zero-drag wing surface radiators on the S5, Mitchell was certain that this was the appropriate method to use on the S6. However, as the 1929 'R' developed over twice the power of the Lion (considerably more than Rolls-Royce had guaranteed) and the effective area of the wing radiators had only increased by about 56% to 235sq ft on the S6, there was a potential problem ahead. Mitchell believed that he had designed the wing radiators to be capable of dissipating the equivalent of 750hp while the RAE suggested that it was likely to be no more

ABOVE The corrugated oil coolers were bolted to the fuselage sides leaving a small air gap. The thin copper tongues were added to the S6B coolers to improve heat transfer.

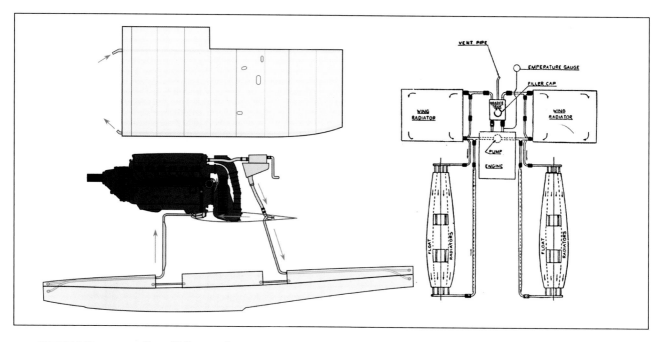

ABOVE S6B water system.

than 680hp, yet it was now estimated that the 'R' would dump heat equivalent of around 860hp into the water. However, wind tunnel tests of the S5 radiators had suggested that they would only be able to dissipate around 65% of the heat from the Lion engine and this had proved to be incorrect, the difference most likely due to uncertainties in the method of extrapolating the test results to race speed. As a consequence there was some reason to believe that the new estimate for the S6 may also have been unduly low. It was also hoped that the greater cooling capacity of the oil system would alleviate some of the possible shortfall, but that was to prove overly optimistic.

The radiator panels were constructed from 6ft x 2ft sheets of 24G Duralumin. The radiators, one each for the top and bottom of the wing, were assembled from an inner and outer panel of joined sheets. A $\frac{1}{16}$in gap between these sheets was maintained by strips of Langite, a product of cork impregnated with shellac, along the lapped and $\frac{3}{32}$in riveted sheet joins, and by flanges on the punched and drilled holes on the outer sheet. These holes were for the eyelets and $\frac{1}{8}$in rivets that joined the skins and were spaced at 2in intervals. The action of riveting brought the flange down against the inner sheet and crimped the eyelet to form a seal and to maintain the required sheet spacing. The lapped joins on the upper and lower surfaces were offset and the Langite strips also served to form chord-wise baffles in the radiator to aid an even flow of water. The inner wing skins had span-wise corrugations at the nose and towards the tail that served as outlet and inlet channels respectively for the

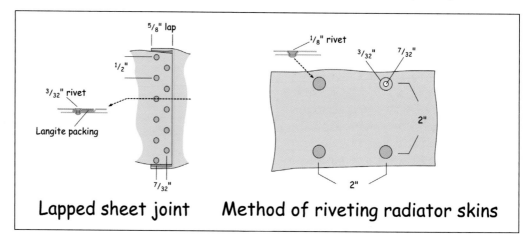

RIGHT Construction details of the wing surface radiators. The float radiators were similar.

Lapped sheet joint   Method of riveting radiator skins

RIGHT Part of a wing surface radiator showing
the multitude of rivets and access ports.

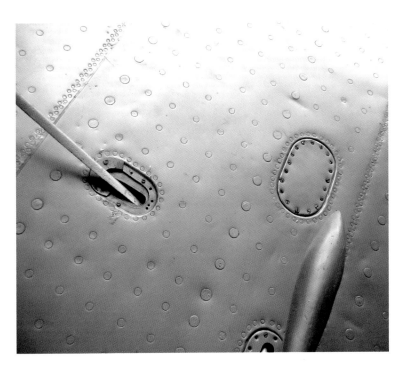

water. As the inlet channel was some distance
from the rear of the radiator and the water flowed
forward, it left a considerable area to the rear
essentially ineffective for cooling. A drain plug
was located in the outer surface at the wing tip
end of the inlet channel. Hand-sized holes had
to be incorporated into the radiator panels to
allow passage of the wing bracing wires and for
access to the aileron control cables and cranks.
The periphery of each hole was sealed by Langite
and close-spaced rivets. Each radiator was
assembled in a jig, the skins, which had been
rolled to the wing profile, were drilled, punched
and then riveted together and the screw holes
and eyelets accurately positioned to match
the corresponding holes in the wing ribs. The
radiators covered the entire surface of the wing
with the exception of the tips and were held in
place by screws. Each radiator was perforated by
thousands of rivet and screw holes, and although
they had measures in place to form a seal, minor
leaks were inevitable. It took around two days
to install the radiator panels on to a wing so, to
ensure there were no unnecessary delays should
repairs be required, sets of replacement wings
were kept in readiness.

In early testing it was soon shown that
the wing radiators did not provide adequate
cooling and the engine could not be run at full
throttle. In the limited time remaining before the
1929 contest two remedies were considered:
a change of coolant to ethylene glycol, or the
fabrication of additional radiators. A quantity
of ethylene glycol was provided by the RAE
to replace the water, not an easy process as
it was far from straightforward to drain all the
water from the engine and the radiators. After
flushing the system with a couple of gallons of
ethylene glycol to drive out the residual water
it was refilled and a ground engine test-run
made at a coolant outlet temperature of 100°C.
Numerous external leaks were observed but
it was unclear whether these were greater

ABOVE Corrugations towards the rear of the inner skin of the wing radiator
formed input channels (waterways shown in red). Water flowed forward so
part of the radiator to the rear was largely ineffective.

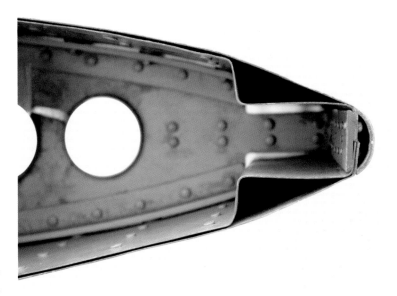

RIGHT Corrugations in the nose of the inner skin
of the wing radiator formed output channels.

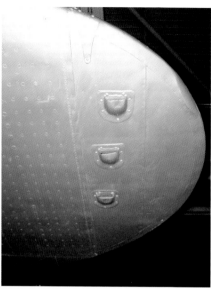

than with water as, unlike water, the ethylene glycol did not evaporate and hence any leak was therefore more visible. There were concerns from Supermarine that the coolant was detrimental to the joints and Heldite sealant used in the radiators; and from Rolls-Royce, who had similar reservations about its effect on the engine connections and seals. Therefore, the runs were terminated and the system restored to water, which meant the tests were inconclusive. It had also been decided to provide cooling to the inner surfaces of the wing radiators by creating a span-wise airflow in the interior of the wing, which was possible as the ribs had been fabricated with large lightening holes. Three small scoops were added to the lower wing surface at the tips that channelled air into the wing interior between the spars. A series of outlet vents were provided in the upper surface wing fairing adjacent to the fuselage. The air velocity within the wing was calculated

BELOW The additional radiator surfaces added to the S6 floats – N247 top, N248 bottom.

as 35mph at race speed. No measurements were made of the effectiveness of this method of cooling until 1931 when it was suggested that heat dissipation of up to 47hp per wing may have been achieved, but that some 30% of the benefit was lost through the additional drag that the scoops created. Mitchell then looked at the possibility of adding 46sq ft of additional radiator area to the fuselage and tailplane, although it is hard to see how this could have been achieved; or of adding 40sq ft additional area to the floats, and it was this latter option that was approved. N247 had four oval radiators measuring 10ft x 1ft added to the sides of the floats, while N248 had two curved triangular radiators of approximately the same total area on the nose decking; in both cases they were simply screwed on to the outer skins and stood proud of the surface by about ½in. With these installed there was a definite improvement in cooling, but neither design proved totally sufficient and as a consequence the speed of the aircraft during the 1929 contest was limited by coolant temperature rather than by engine power as it was still not possible to run at maximum revs.

As the decision to enter the 1931 contest was not made until the beginning of February there was no time to design, test and build a completely new cooling system, so the wing radiators had to remain unchanged. For the refurbished S6s, now designated S6A with their enlarged floats, the quick solution was essentially to combine the two radiator types installed in 1929, but it was known that this would be inadequate to deal with the extra power expected from the upgraded 'R' engines. Each float radiator was divided longitudinally into separate left and right units. Water entered at the rear and flowed to the nose where internal baffles reversed the flow back to the outlet pipes located close to the front struts. The return pipe was also part of the cooling system and profiled to form the front of the strut fairing. Some rudimentary aerodynamic fairing of the front lip of the radiator was applied to the nose of the floats.

The S6B had complex surface radiators installed on the new floats. There were five separate radiator panels per float: three on the upper decking – nose, mid and rear – and two along the sides. The whole system effectively covered the entire upper surface with the

exception of the extreme nose and stern, and the inspection hatches around the base of the struts. There were minor variations in the rivet and bolt-hole spacing on the port and starboard float sets on account of the differences in float construction around the small and large fuel tanks. The construction of the radiators required jigs and moulds to ensure accurate alignment of all fittings with those on the float frames and followed the method used for the wings. The skins were of 24G Duralumin and the gap between them ⅛in. The tinned steel fuel tank was recessed slightly so that an insulating air gap of ³⁄₃₂in separated it from the radiators. Each radiator was attached by bolts and screws to the float frames and intercostals. The combined area of the five radiator components on each float was 166sq ft of which 146sq ft was deemed to be effective; the remainder, as in the wing trailing edge, did not benefit from full water flow.

Hot water from the engine was pumped to the span-wise input channels towards the rear of the wing radiators and then flowed forward, constrained by the chord-wise baffles, to the outlet channel in the leading edge and then back to the engine. This was the primary system. A parallel secondary system took water down piping within the rear float strut fairings to inputs in the rear of the float radiators, of which there was one each for the side radiators and two for the upper stern radiator, which had a baffle running down the centre line. The side radiators, constructed in one piece, had a single outlet at the front while the three radiators on the top decking were linked in series by connecting pipes and had twin outlet pipes at the nose. The return piping ran up the leading edge of the front strut fairings and then to the header tank. This was constructed of Duralumin as an integral part of the fuselage in the upper front cockpit and had a capacity of 7gal. It also included a tinned steel steam separator. The total heat dissipation capacity of the system was measured as 990hp, which was not quite sufficient to allow for the prolonged use of full throttle. With the engine running at the maximum revs of 3,200rpm the water temperature rise through the engine was about 83°C relative to the surrounding air temperature, which meant that if the ambient temperature was above 17°C then the water would boil.

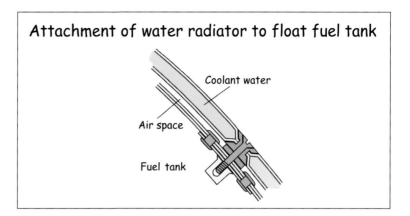

ABOVE The float radiator panels were screwed to the float frames with a small insulating air gap around the fuel tank.

BELOW Float side and top radiators on the S6B showing lap joints, flush riveting and attachment screws. An access panel, secured by multiple screws, can be seen adjacent to the bracing wire.

BOTTOM The closely spaced rivets and screws in the upper float nose radiator gave the panel a quilted surface.

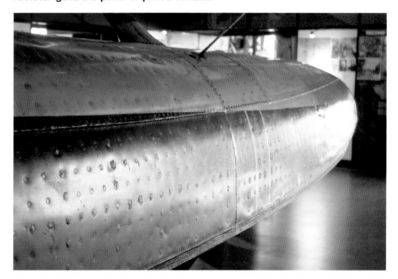

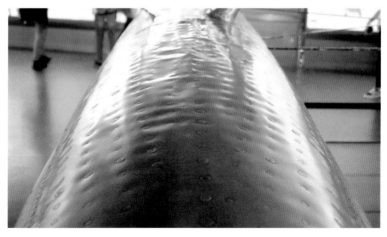

Chapter Five

Flying the S6B and earlier Supermarine racing seaplanes

Considering the small number of pilots who had the opportunity to fly Supermarine's racers and the limited number of flights they were each able to make, a surprising number of accounts have been written about their experiences – several are anecdotal for a general audience, some are in the form of presentations and papers, while others are contained in official reports.

OPPOSITE Richard Atcherley prepares for his first flight in an S6.

ABOVE **The Gloster I was used as a trainer in 1927.**

Accounts of flying the Supermarine seaplane racers provide a valuable insight into the quirks and attributes of these exotic aircraft. All of the British racing seaplanes shared certain characteristics. They were very sensitive to sea state – too smooth and it was often impossible to achieve take-off, too rough and they were dangerously unstable. Most were prone to porpoising unless handled with care, and lateral rocking from float to float was common. By the standards of the era they accelerated and climbed rapidly, and care had to be taken not to pull excessive negative-g when levelling out. The rate of deceleration

when the throttles were closed was low and the approach when landing was lengthy. Techniques mastered in one aircraft were a useful guide when flying another type, but each had its own individual quirks and had to be treated with respect until mastered.

Henry Biard flew the Sea Lion II to victory in 1922, took the Sea Lion III to third place in 1923 and would have flown the S4 in the contest in 1925 had it not been wrecked during the preliminary trials. In the mid-1930s he wrote an autobiography, *Wings,* which could have given an invaluable insight into all these aircraft but unfortunately he wrote to entertain rather than inform. Where his anecdotes can be checked against known facts they fall well short; for example, his account of the 1922 contest is a work of pure fiction. Unfortunately this then throws into doubt his description of his flights in the S4, where he claimed to have had misgivings about the aircraft from the start, noting odd shivers in the wings, visions of being shadowed by a 'ghost' aircraft and experiencing premonitions of trouble ahead. As no other pilot flew the aircraft its characteristics remain unknown.

The period of aircraft test flights prior to the 1927 contest is described in some detail by Harry Schofield in his autobiography, *The*

RIGHT **Both Gloster IIIs were modified and used for training and research in 1927; they were not well liked.**

THE RAF HIGH SPEED FLIGHT

When Air Vice-Marshal Salmond initiated the high speed aircraft research programme it was agreed that a specialised RAF High Speed Flight (HSF) should be created to take responsibility for the test flights of the new aircraft, to undertake high-speed flying research and, should entry for the 1927 Schneider Trophy contest be approved, to pilot the competing aircraft. The unit would be appended to the MAEE at Felixstowe.

The pilots for the HSF were selected based on their experience flying a broad variety of aircraft types, which meant that those who had served as test pilots at the RAE, the AAEE evaluation unit or the MAEE, or had been instructors at the Central Flying School (CFS), tended to be favoured. A shortlist of pilots were invited to put their names forward but It does not appear to be recorded how the initial recommendations were made or who was ultimately responsible for making the final selection.

Flt Lt Oswald Worsley, who was on the staff at the MAEE, was named as the first pilot officer to join in the summer of 1926 and command was placed in the hands of Sqn Ldr Leonard Slatter a little later, but it would be some time before the next pilots, Flg Off Rex Stocken and Flt Lt John Chick, were to join. Both were seasoned and competent fliers but Slatter was not satisfied and submitted a request for additional pilots. When Stocken had the misfortune to have the Gloster IIIB capsize while under tow he was dismissed and Flg Off Sidney Webster, a test pilot at the AAEE, and Flg Off Harry Schofield, a CFS flight instructor, then joined. When Chick spent the best part of two weeks attempting to get the Gloster IV into the air he, too, left and Flt Lt Samuel Kinkead replaced him. At the same time, and surprisingly late in proceedings, the HSF was strengthened by the assignment of their own Technical Officer, Flg Off Tom Moon, from the staff at the MAEE. A support crew of NCOs and airmen, selected from the best available in the RAF's front-line squadrons, was allocated to the HSF to handle and maintain the racing and training aircraft. They generally numbered between 10 and 20, depending on the number of aircraft.

Trenchard had always expressed reservations about the formation of an elite HSF, which would elevate the status of the pilots in the public eye, something to which he was vehemently opposed believing it to be detrimental to morale in the force. There was, however, nothing he could do about it and the press and public did indeed welcome the pilots

LEFT The 1927 High Speed Flight (HSF): Flt Lts Schofield and Worseley, Flg Off Webster, Flt Lt Kinkead and Sqn Ldr Slatter.

ABOVE **Ground crew of the HSF in 1927.** *(Jonathan Falconer)*

ABOVE RIGHT **Sqn Ldr Augustus Orlebar, the highly regarded commanding officer of the HSF from 1929 to 1931.**

returning from the 1927 contest as national heroes, turning out in large numbers when they arrived back at Croydon Airport. Trenchard's response was to disband the HSF immediately. This decision was questioned in many quarters and eventually overturned.

Kinkead was recalled in 1928 to prepare for an attempt at the absolute air speed record, but this ended in tragedy when he flew the S5 into the water at high speed and was killed, the first fatality that the HSF had experienced. The conclusions of the accident inquiry certainly had no impact on the plans of the HSF, which prepared for another record attempt later in the year. Flt Lt David D'Arcy Greig joined in May. On 4 November he made six runs over the speed course and established a mean speed that exceeded the record held by Italy, but by a margin insufficient to be accepted as a world record.

Shortly before Greig's record attempt three new pilots, Flg Offs Chris Staniland and Richard Atcherley, and Flt Lt George Stainforth, were assigned to the HSF to prepare for the 1929 contest, and it was announced that Sqn Ldr Augustus Orlebar would become the new commanding officer. Staniland's posting was cancelled when it was discovered that his service commission was due to expire, so they were joined in January 1929 by Flg Off Henry Waghorn. Unlike the 1927 team, who were not closely acquainted, these four pilots had served together in the CFS in 1927.

Orlebar arrived in January 1929 to take command but for the early weeks he ran the HSF jointly with Greig until such time as he himself had learned the ways of seaplanes and racers. In April the HSF moved to Calshot and by the early summer they were all quite familiar with the training aircraft and the contest course, so Atcherley and Stainforth could be released to enter the King's Cup race in a two-seat Gloster Grebe, and they won.

Orlebar took it upon himself to make all the early test flights with each new aircraft as they were delivered. The question of who was to fly which aircraft in the contest had been discussed with the team prior to their delivery and the test-flying schedule was arranged accordingly. Waghorn and Atcherley were assigned the S6s and Stainforth the Gloster VI, leaving Greig as the team reserve with the S5.

After the contest and speed record runs Waghorn, Atcherley and Greig were reassigned while Orlebar and Stainforth returned to the MAEE. However, Stainforth left shorty after and was replaced by Flt Lt John Boothman, who undertook the limited flying for the research programme in 1930. Flt Lts Francis Long and Eustace Hope joined later. The Gloster IV was pensioned off early in the year and the Gloster IVB was wrecked when Boothman lost control on landing. The engines in the Gloster VIs could never be persuaded to run reliably.

When government support was granted for the 1931 contest the pilots of the HSF were selected. Under Orlebar's leadership Boothman, Long and Hope were joined by Stainforth, who had been recalled, and new recruits Flg Offs Leonard Snaith and Haliburton Leech, and

LEFT The 1929 HSF
with Henry Royce:
Flg Offs Atcherley and
Waghorn, Sqn Ldr
Orlebar, Flt Lt Greig,
Flg Off Moon and
Flt Lt Stainforth.

Lt Gerald Brinton from the Royal Navy. Flt Lt Dry, an engineering officer at the MAEE, took responsibility for the aircraft. The team was now unnecessarily large so Brinton and Leech were dropped, but Brinton was recalled later following Hope's accident.

The HSF was well equipped with hack and training aircraft and should have had an easy time preparing for the contest, yet the serious damage incurred by the S6A, N247, on its first flight was followed by the sinking of its sister racer, N248, and the fatal crash on take-off by Brinton in the rebuilt N247. Boothman, Long and Snaith were selected for the contest, although only Boothman flew. Stainforth was allocated the task of making two attempts, both successful, on the world absolute speed record and the HSF was disbanded immediately after these were completed.

In 1946 the HSF was re-formed in order to set new world speed records with the RAF's new Gloster Meteor jet fighter.

LEFT The 1931 HSF:
Flt Lt Hope,
Lt Brinton RN, Flt Lts
Long and Stainforth,
Sqn Ldr Orlebar,
Flt Lt Boothman, Flg
Off Snaith, Flt Lt Dry.

ABOVE The Gloster IV was notorious for the poor view from the cockpit. The Gloster IVA and IVB were an improvement but still inferior to the Supermarine S5.

BELOW The Short-Bristow Crusader handled well, but erratic airflow into the supercharger resulted in violent engine misfires and cut-outs.

High Speed and Other Flights, also written in the mid-1930s. While his writing style is deliberately non-technical it is factually correct and his views on flying the aircraft appear to be commendably objective. He was able to fly the Gloster I, Gloster IIIA, IV and IVA, the Short-Bristow Crusader and the S5, and gave his impressions of flying each of them. The Gloster IIIA was unpredictably unstable in yaw and the Gloster IV suffered from extremely poor visibility and shipped a lot of spray. The supercharger on the Crusader's Mercury engine was prone to cutting in and out, which resulted in violent deceleration, acceleration and twisting of the airframe. These negative experiences obviously coloured Schofield's perception of the S5, which he found positively benign in comparison. He described the visibility from the cockpit as infinitely better than that from the Gloster IV, it suffered less from spray but had a longer take-off run and he found it rather difficult to become airborne. In the air the aircraft was responsive and well balanced. As one of the stockier pilots he found the cockpit to be very cramped indeed, especially as arms and legs had to be held clear of the fuselage sides because

LEFT The first
Supermarine Napier
S5, N219, is rolled out
for an early test flight.

the oil coolers made these extremely hot. The
canopy, even with the wind deflectors around
its edges, was barely large enough and care
had to be taken not to lean to either side into
the slipstream. Fumes and soot from the central
cylinder bank would enter the cockpit when
making a left turn.

D'Arcy Greig's autobiography, *My Golden
Flying Years*, was written in his retirement and
published posthumously. His first experience
flying a racing seaplane came in the summer
of 1928 in the Gloster IV after it had been
adapted as a trainer by raising the top wing to
improve visibility. As a consequence of all the

BELOW All three
Gloster IVs had their
top wings raised to
improve visibility.

ABOVE The Gloster IVA and IVB were fitted with the fin and rudder design from the IV. They handled well and were even rolled and looped.

changes he did not suffer the same negative impression of the aircraft as had the HSF pilots in 1927. When the Gloster IVA arrived he found that it suffered badly from instability in yaw, and as this had not been experienced with the Gloster IV it was returned to GAC to be refitted with the fin and rudder design from

this aircraft; the Gloster IVB was modified in the same way. Greig says very little about the S5's handling on the water or in the air but goes to some length to describe the cramped cockpit, the heat from the oil coolers and the ingress of exhaust. After flying the S5, N219, in the 1929 contest his face was completely

RIGHT The Supermarine Napier S5 was well liked by the pilots and served with the HSF until 1931.

blackened by the exhaust and he was partially deaf for a few days from the noise of the engine. The Napier Lion VIID had the exhaust ports moved to the other side of the central cylinders to address the fume problem.

Webster's comments in his log book after his first flight in an S5 said simply 'very, very nice'. Waghorn noted that the aircraft would quiver at the stall and a wing would flick down. He found the torque effect on left turns tiring, which may have been due in part to the asymmetric offset of the floats. Stainforth mentioned the cramped cockpit, that the rudder bar was too close to the seat and during take-off the right knee and elbow competed for space. Snaith flew the aircraft in 1931, by which time it was becoming distinctly worn, leaky, and prone to odd vibrations and slack in the controls.

In 1929 the pilots had plenty of opportunity to familiarise themselves with the general qualities of high-speed seaplanes prior to the contest flying the modified Gloster IVs and Supermarine S5s. They had all acquired plenty of experience of the shared characteristics of the aircraft – the lack of forward view, the torque effects when accelerating on the water, heavy spray entering the cockpit, prolonged take-off runs, high G turns and so on, so that when the S6s arrived all of these factors were taken for granted and it was just the idiosyncrasies specific to this aircraft that had to be mastered. In 1931, with the S6A and S6B the situation was much the same.

Orlebar, Waghorn, Stainforth, Boothman and Snaith have all left written descriptions of flying the S6 series aircraft, and the techniques developed for flying the S6, S6A and S6B were broadly the same with just minor variations.

Taxiing and take-off run

With the engine throttled right back it was possible to taxi and turn in a light wind with the application of quick bursts of power, but the time taken doing this had to be kept as short as possible otherwise fuel would begin to pool in the supercharger plenum and on opening the throttle the rich mixture entering the engine would cause misfires and, in the worst cases, wash away the lubricant in the cylinders and cause damage. The technique

established for take-off was to point the aircraft some 45° to 70° to the right of the wind and apply full right rudder and stick, back and to the right. On opening the throttle the cockpit was engulfed by spray until the aircraft reached around 30mph and began to rise on to the float step. The S6 was particularly bad through

RIGHT As the S6 accelerates the nose rises and the massive torque effect drives the port float down.

RIGHT Once running on the float steps the spray clears. The nose had to be kept high to prevent porpoising.

BELOW The S6B riding cleanly on the float steps.

this stage as the floats had insufficient reserve buoyancy and the heels would submerge, adding drag and raising the nose of the aircraft excessively. It was advisable for the pilot to lean well forward and keep his head down under the canopy to avoid the worst of the spray for the first few seconds. At around 40 to 50mph the controls became effective and the pilot had to use the rudder carefully to coax the aircraft into wind without letting it swing too far, which it was prone to do, as it was all but impossible to pull it back if it veered to the left of the wind. Once into the wind the nose dropped as the aircraft rose on to the float steps and it would continue to accelerate until leaving the water at around 100mph, or slightly higher for the heavier S6B. The aircraft ran on the water at a flatter angle than the S5, which was always

particularly nose high. It was important to keep the stick held fully back throughout the take-off phase to prevent porpoising, despite the natural urge to ease forward as it left the water at a high angle of attack. If violent porpoising did develop it was difficult to get back under control and the aircraft would not accelerate, so it was advisable to close the throttles and start again. In 1929 Atcherley did manage to quell the porpoising of S6, N248, while taking off for the contest, but during the struggle and rollercoaster ride in the cockpit he lost his goggles and had to fly without them. In more disturbed water it was occasionally possible to ease the stick forward slightly at speeds above 80mph to prevent the aircraft jumping into the air at too steep an angle. The take-off run was generally between 30 and 40 seconds.

LEFT A sequence of movie frames showing Atcherley's take-off run in N248 for the 1929 contest. The aircraft is starting to porpoise in the last two frames.

Take-off and flight

Take-off was usually rather sudden and at a high angle, but acceleration remained slow as the propeller was still stalled. It was essential to keep the stick pulled back to avoid sinking back on to the water, although both Waghorn in the S6 and Stainforth in the S6A found it very difficult to take off cleanly at full load and bounced lightly a couple of times. It was a momentary lapse in following the instruction to keep the stick right back that resulted in Brinton's fatal crash when making his first flight in S6A, N247. Elevator control was strong and had to be handled with care as the aircraft was prone to a degree of longitudinal instability if it was even slightly out of trim. As speed increased all controls became effective, the rudder and elevators being generally light and the ailerons a little heavy. If the rigging and trim had been set correctly then it was possible to fly level hands-off at high speed, but as the oil and fuel load decreased the change in centre of gravity, both longitudinally and laterally, was very noticeable and the load on the control stick to maintain level flight could become tiring.

Turning and g-load

During the test-flight phase in 1927 the pilots had concluded that a turn producing an acceleration of between 5 and 6g appeared the best approach, but research into the optimal method was carried out more thoroughly with the Gloster IV and S5 in 1929 and 1930 and then repeated in 1931 with the S6A. Several methods of measuring the turn were tried but the simplest was found to be for the pilot to fly towards Calshot castle at high speed and at right angles to the shoreline and then initiate a left turn. The position along the beach where he completed the turn was noted by an observer with a stopwatch in a boat some distance offshore. The shoreline had been 'calibrated' beforehand by measuring the distance of various trees, huts etc, from the castle.

Turns were made of various radii and the g-load in the aircraft measured with an accelerometer. These tests had shown that a level smooth curve with an acceleration of between 3 and 6g resulted in the least loss of speed and about 4g was found most acceptable by the pilots. For the S6B the optimal turn had a diameter of about 1,200yd and the method adopted for the contest was to approach the turn marker running about 800yd to the right of the mean course line. A line had been painted on the port wing running from the pilot's eye-line outwards at 45° and when this aligned with the marker the turn was initiated and the aircraft pulled into a near vertical bank. In this way the aircraft would pass just outside the marker at the apex of the turn.

ABOVE The moment of take-off for Boothman in the heavily loaded S6B.

BELOW The Supermarine Rolls-Royce S6B in flight.

RIGHT A series of
measured turns were
made over Calshot at
high speed in order to
ascertain the optimal
turn radius and
acceleration.

The aircraft had a tendency to climb slightly at the start of the turn due to aileron drag, which had to be compensated for by the application of rudder; however, some pilots felt that this extra drag slowed the aircraft and so allowed the height to rise slightly during the turn. The correct longitudinal position of the centre of gravity was particularly important when turning, because if it was even just a little to the rear the stick had to be held firmly with forward pressure to prevent it from flicking fully backwards. This was found to be quite tricky to maintain.

Approach and landing

Stall speed of the S6, at 95mph, was about the same as that of the S5; for the heavier S6B it was considerably higher at 110 to 115mph when fully loaded. The stall was gentle and occurred without prior warning and without dropping a wing. Because of the lack of forward vision the approach to a landing had to be initiated at least two miles out and made across wind to be able to select a touchdown point and clear line into wind. The approach was flown at

RIGHT The wing root
of S6A, N248, following
Hope's landing
accident.

118
SUPERMARINE ROLLS-ROYCE S6B MANUAL

RIGHT **Frames from the film of the S6A at the moment of touchdown. As at take-off the nose had to be held high.** *(Crown Copyright)*

about 160mph, at which speed the attitude of the aircraft was slightly nose high and the rate of sink quite rapid. Over a mile from the selected touchdown point and flying into wind the engine was throttled back and the aircraft levelled out in order to assess the height above the water, and then allowed to descend. With the throttle closed the stick was slowly brought back until the angle of attack was roughly the same as that at take-off and the water touched with the heels of the floats at a speed of around 110mph, or higher if loaded. The stick had to be held right back to prevent pitching forward, which would result in it either jumping back into the air or the noses of the floats plunging. Any tendency to swing had to be checked by applying coarse rudder. As the floats touched down the increasing water drag slowed the aircraft rapidly, and when it came down off the float steps the nose dropped and it came to a fairly abrupt stop.

Flt Lt Hope lost control of S6A, N248, after a test flight prior to the 1931 contest when he touched the wake of a passing ship on landing and was thrown back into the air. The aircraft fell on to the water, flipped over and sank, but thankfully Hope struggled free having suffered only bruising and a punctured eardrum. Flt Lt Stainforth had a similar accident in S6B, S1596, while testing propellers. In his case the heel of his shoe jammed under the rudder pedal and the aircraft cartwheeled. He, too, got free before the aircraft sank.

For an attempt on an absolute speed record the FAI set strict rules that had to be adhered to throughout the flight. The maximum altitude that could be flown at any time was 400m (1,312ft) and the 3km (1.86 miles) speed run course had to be flown at an altitude of no more than 50m (164ft). At 500m (1,640ft) before and beyond the speed course the aircraft had to be flying level. This left the opportunity to dive into the speed course and for the S6B it was determined that the best angle for this dive was 15°. To aid the pilot in diving at the correct angle a black line was painted on to the cockpit window, which when aligned with the horizon ensured that the aircraft was flying at the correct attitude.

Chapter Six

Preparing and maintaining the S6B

As a thoroughbred racing machine the S6B and its Rolls-Royce engine required the dedicated attention of highly-skilled and specialised engineers working long hours.

OPPOSITE Developing and maintaining the S6 racers and their engines was a 24-hour process. S6, N248, at Calshot in 1929.

121

Development and servicing

All racing seaplanes were designed for a short service life and for flights lasting well under an hour. In the limited time between their first flight and the contest they were almost always subject to a series of upgrades and modifications, some carried out on site and others requiring a return to the manufacturer. Several of the aircraft were subsequently retained on the active list, either revised for use as trainers or overhauled as back-up racers for later contests, but none saw great use. In all cases maintenance was a quite different affair from that of a standard service aircraft and evolved along with the aircraft. Some of this was handled by the technical crew attached to the HSF, but most was the responsibility of the aircraft and engine manufacturers – a mixture of modifications, repairs and pre-flight preparation.

Ease of access to serviceable parts was a secondary consideration for Supermarine in the design of the S6B and the numerous covers, caps and removable panels were secured in place by closely spaced small screws. None were particularly large and several were difficult to reach. Maintenance was a frustrating and time-consuming procedure.

For handling on land each aircraft came with its own dedicated wheeled trolley and trestles. On the trolley, padded supports were shaped to fit the floats with the fore and aft pairs spaced to match those of the robust float bulkheads to which the struts were secured. Vertical white lines were painted on the sides of the floats to indicate where the trolley should be positioned. For added stability, crossbars were often fitted between the towing eyes on the floats and provided a useful anchorage point for restraining

BELOW The S6B was manoeuvred ashore on a dedicated wheeled trolley positioned under strong points on the floats. Spreader bars fitted to the towing eyes aided stability. *(C. Michell)*

LEFT Aeronautical Inspection Directorate (AID) inspector E.L. Ransome, far right, and Rolls-Royce engineer Cyril Lovesey, in light trousers, supervise the installation of the 'R' engine perched on planks between stepladders.

ropes when the engine was run on land or the aircraft was lowered down the slipway. When stationary, simple shaped trestles were placed under the bow and stern of the floats.

All maintenance onshore would take place with the aircraft on the trolley. It was possible to sit on the S6B's floats, with weight carefully distributed to avoid denting the radiators, but standing was only possible on the access panels adjacent to the struts and at the nose. To reach the cockpit a special ladder hooked over the dorsal spine and rested against the float side, suitably padded. It was just feasible, with care, to place a foot on the wing root, inboard of the radiator. To work on the engine or propeller basic platforms were set up using robust planks supported on stepladders, although it appears that special platforms were also built which fitted over the inner wing.

On the S6B the fuel system initially proved troublesome as a consequence of the solvent action of the methanol and acetone that constituted part of the fuel mixture for the contest and speed records respectively. Surplus jointing compound in the system also dissolved and the only recourse, as Mitchell told the HSF, was to run the engines until the residue was flushed out. This often took several flights to clear. When the fine filters on the fuel lines within the float tanks became clogged with hair

and fluff they were found to be very difficult to access and clean. These filters were replaced by simple gauze screens sufficient to trap coarser material such as small metal particles. The source of the fluff proved to be, in part, the flexible hoses manufactured by Superflexit, which were being degraded by the fuel. They were replaced by Petroflex hoses manufactured by Hobdell, Way & Co.

The complex system of wing and float radiators, 14 in all, had to be cleared of trapped air by bleeding through drain plugs. However, these were not always located in easily accessible positions and several were not at the high point of the radiator and hence not ideal to remove the air. Those on the wings were considered to be too close to the tips and one on the floats required the removal of some 200 small screws to gain access. Experience showed that the best method to clear the air was to raise the nose of the aircraft as high as possible, open the wing tip vents and run water into the header tank by hose for about 30 minutes.

Minor water seepage through the radiators' many joints and rivet holes was common but the volume lost was negligible. The proprietary motoring radiator sealant 'Neverleak' was added to the water with moderate success.

The oil system was largely trouble free. The oil filter was reached through an access port

PREPARING AND MAINTAINING THE S6B

ABOVE Lovesey and
his team work on the
'R' engine watched
by Ransome. Oil is
being drained from
the cooler under the
nose. Numerous water
droplets under the
wing water radiator
are testament to the
seepage.

in the fuselage side and the filler was a similar port high in the fin. Drain plugs were located in both the side and ventral coolers, and were usually bled from the front. As the castor oil had a rather high viscosity it was pre-heated and the system filled just prior to flight to avoid any possibility of the oil coolers rupturing.

The S6 had proven to be a little unstable longitudinally, which was one reason why it was prone to porpoising. The S6B was worse and very sensitive to the position of the centre of gravity. The greater oil load in the fin tank added to the instability. When the mass balances were added to the rudder, exacerbating the problem, it was reskinned with fabric to reduce the weight but the only remedy to bring the centre of gravity forward was to add lead weights in the bows of the floats. Weights totalling 50lb or more were required, with the mass carefully calculated and based on the fuel load, the weight of the pilot and the minor differences between aircraft.

RIGHT Each of the
three corrugated oil
coolers had a small
drain plug at front and
rear.

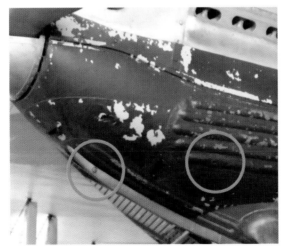

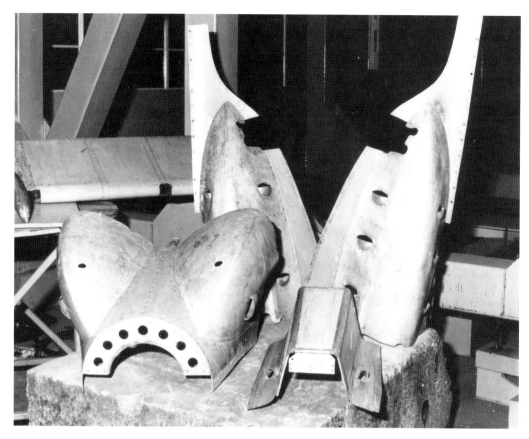

LEFT The fore and aft
cylinder bank fairings
screwed directly
to the engine and
occasionally buckled
due to vibration and
thermal expansion.
(C. Michell)

The trim of the control surfaces was set up to the preference of the pilot after he had made a preliminary flight with full fuel and oil loads. Thin alloy trim strips on the trailing edges of the elevators and rudder were bent on the ground, based on the pilot's reports on control stick loads during flight. The tension in the control cables could be checked and adjusted from the connections in the cockpit and rear of the engine bay, both requiring a degree of contortion by the engineer. Further checks of the rudder and elevator connections were achieved by removing the tail fairing under the rudder, and of the ailerons through the small access panels in the upper wing radiators.

During testing a number of problems occurred with fairing panels that required modification or the fabrication of replacement parts. In 1931 some of the engine cowl panels buckled due to thermal expansion and required adjustment. The cuff fairings at the top of the float struts fractured on a number of flights as a result of the securing screws loosening due to buffeting from the high-speed slipstream behind the propeller. Improved fixings were fabricated.

In 1929 Rolls-Royce had allocated two engines to each aircraft and these were swapped out after about one hour in the air at high or full throttle. The engines were returned to the Rolls-Royce factory in Derby on a cradle installed on the rear of the chassis of a Phantom car. In the factory the engine was completely stripped down, thoroughly checked and rebuilt, upgraded parts from the continuing development programme were incorporated and any time-expired components replaced. After a bench test the engine was ready to

LEFT The fairing cuffs
at the top of the struts
took a battering from
the slipstream and the
securing screws were
prone to loosening.

be returned. With the S6 it could take several days to complete an engine change, but with experience this was cut down considerably, although two days was generally considered the best that could be achieved. As the engine was a very tight fit in the airframe very little adjustment or maintenance could be carried out once it was installed. It was a feat of some magnitude, therefore, that the Rolls-Royce team managed to remove and replace an entire cylinder block on the engine in N247 during the night before the 1929 contest.

For the early racers the usual practice had been to launch from a sheltered slipway and then taxi away and take off directly. But as their performance increased the need for a large area of open, calm water became essential and they had to be towed behind motor tenders to a convenient location. This was far from ideal as

they were a little unstable as a consequence of the low reserve buoyancy of the floats, making it difficult for the pilot to climb in with the aircraft afloat, and the support crew were unable to carry out any work that may have been required. It was therefore decided that some form of support and launch vessel was required, so in the summer of 1929 Saunders-Roe were contracted to build three floating platforms to carry the seaplanes, for which a design was prepared in conjunction with the aptly named Mr Launchbury of the Air Ministry Technical Development Department. The pontoon was like a small floating dock, 41ft long and 13ft 6in wide, capable of taking on a seaplane and shipping it overboard again quickly. A V-bottom hull was produced in metal with a watertight deck fairly close to the keel. The stern end of the hull was left open to the sea and the bow

BELOW Once installed in the aircraft it was difficult to access many of the ancillaries and pipework connectors on the engine. Removal and replacement was a laborious process.
(C. Michell)

end raised and decked over to form a shelter for the HSF mechanics to stow their gear or retreat from the rain. This was enclosed by a steel watertight bulkhead and from this to the after-end of the hull a watertight steel deck fitted with rollers was built at about the level of the waterline. A chassis was made of steel angle bars covered with wood decking, which sat on top of the rollers forming a movable platform.

Preparations for flight

Preparing the S6B for a flight was relatively simple but nevertheless time-consuming. There was a series of standard checks and procedures to carry out after which each aircraft had to be set up to suit the particular engine installed and the personal preferences of the pilot.

The bracing wire rigging was checked for tension and alignment and adjusted as required. A rule of thumb was established whereby about a 10' change in incidence was required to adjust for each pound of side-load on the stick. For the streamline wires an alignment error of 5° resulted in an increase in drag of 25%, and as the bracing was responsible for 16% of the total aircraft drag this had to be minimised. It

was found that once set the rigging gave little trouble; breakages had not been uncommon with the S5, but the revised system on the S6s had resolved this. The fuel system was thoroughly cleaned and the fuel tanks filled via a cloth filter in a funnel to ensure no foreign matter was introduced. Fuel was either poured directly from 1gal cans or more usually by hand pump from drums. The quantity to be placed in each float had been determined beforehand based on the expected duration of the flight and the lateral offset load required. The water system was bled from the wing tip drains to remove any air and then topped up. The oil, warmed in a Zwicky heater, was poured into the fin tank and bled through the drains at the nose of each cooler. The cover over the supercharger intake was removed and the engine could then be started using an external starter unit, the fuel mixture lever was set by the Rolls-Royce engineer and locked, and the aircraft launched. If it was necessary to tow the aircraft out to sea on a launching pontoon, the starter, oil heater and associated filling equipment would be placed on board.

When a new engine had been installed it was normal to make the first flight using a set

ABOVE **Ransome, Boothman and Lovesey relax on the foredeck of the launch pontoon, a simple metal barge, open at the rear.** (C. Michell)

OPPOSITE The float fuel tanks of the S6B are filled from drums using a small hand pump, a funnel and filter cloth.

ABOVE The S6 is prepared for a flight. The oil drain plug at the nose is being checked and the pipes from the RAE compressed air starter have been connected.

BELOW After the S6 has been launched from the slipway a pinnace prepares to tow it to the pontoon anchored a short distance offshore.

of 'practice' spark plugs. After a ground test, where the Rolls-Royce engineer checked the systems and set the mixture controls, a short test flight was made with a light fuel load. After the flight the plugs were removed and the cylinder bores inspected. New plugs were then fitted. Sets of plugs were returned to the makers, Lodge, after a flight to be checked for damage, especially cracking of the insulator, where they were reconditioned and returned for use. For the contest the oil and boost pressure gauge connectors at the engine were blanked off as a precaution in case of failure of the pipes.

If the launching pontoon was to be used it was moved close to the slipway where a motor launch would tow the aircraft the short distance to the waiting HSF crew. The aircraft was located over the platform, secured, and the platform winched back on to the pontoon and locked in place. A pinnace towed the pontoon to the selected take-off location where it dropped anchor, the pinnace waiting nearby.

The engine was primed with dope through the exhaust ports and a gas starter connected to the input pipes located under a cover in the fuselage side behind the pilot's right shoulder. Two types of starter were tried: the Bristol starter, which used a two-stroke fuel; and the RAE compressed-air-bottle starter that fed a mixture of air and petrol. The latter was preferred as the lubricant in the Bristol's fuel could foul the plugs, as could the priming dope. It was essential to keep all connections in the starter's piping and electrical circuits free from seawater contamination and that air used to recharge the bottles was dry. These precautions minimised the possibility of the engine failing to start on the first attempt, which increased the likelihood of the plugs becoming fouled and needing to be changed. Once the engine was running smoothly the pilot boarded, strapped in and the platform was lowered to release the aircraft. The whole operation from slipway to take-off would take at least an hour.

BELOW The engine of the S6 has been started by the Rolls-Royce team and Waghorn climbs aboard ready to be launched from the pontoon. S6, N247, in 1929.

After landing the engine was switched off as soon as the aircraft completed its landing run and a motor pinnace would race to the scene to take it in tow. It was usually towed back directly to the slipway for recovery, although the pontoon was available if required. The pilot was carried ashore by a member of the crew in waders before the aircraft was manoeuvred over the handling trolley and pulled back up the slipway. This operation took a minimum of half an hour to complete.

ABOVE At the end of a flight the S6 is taken in tow by a pinnace.

LEFT The undignified end to a flight as the pilot, in this case Orlebar, is carried ashore by one of the HSF support crew.

131

Chapter Seven

The Schneider Trophy Contest of 1931 – a dismal finale

Uncertainty, dithering and intransigence almost scuppered Britain's defence of the Schneider Trophy in 1931, but all was saved at the last moment by a generous private donation and the all-out efforts of Rolls-Royce and Supermarine.

OPPOSITE Prime Minister Ramsay MacDonald addresses the assembled guests at the RAeC dinner aboard the SS *Orford*. His speech was taken to imply that government funding would be forthcoming for 1931.

Back-to-back wins in 1927 and 1929 had been achieved with dominant aircraft and engines, a comprehensive research and development programme that had more than justified the expense, and a specialised group of highly trained RAF pilots. All seemed set for a fantastic conclusion to the contest in 1931. What could possibly go wrong?

At the RAeC dinner following the British success at the 1929 contest, Prime Minister Ramsay MacDonald was reported to have said in his speech that 'We are going to do our level best to win again.' On 30 October, after the Wall Street Crash had acted as the catalyst that initiated the collapse of the world economy, the RAeC received a letter from the Air Ministry informing them that there would be no support of any kind forthcoming for the 1931 contest, and a statement was also released to the press. Within the Air Ministry the feeling was that the high-speed research programme had run its course and there was no benefit to be derived from entering a further contest. Unwisely the RAeC took no action, leaving it until the very end of 1930 before giving serious consideration to the implications, presumably blithely assuming that the decision would be reversed.

However, the RAeC did take steps to tighten up the rules for the 1931 contest to try and ensure that it would take place on the specified date. The navigability trials on the day preceding the speed contest were to be abandoned and the criteria for postponing the contest firmed up. In addition, the entry fee was to be raised substantially to minimise the possibility of countries submitting entries for a team only to push for a delay and then forfeit at the very last moment, as had happened in 1929. The elaborate and costly preparations by the government, host towns, railways, BBC and a plethora of others had been based on the assumption that four nations would compete with ten aircraft between them to provide an unmissable spectacle, yet it had come so close to Britain flying alone unchallenged. After months of dispute and legal argument the FAI reluctantly agreed to the changes and that the refundable entry deposit would rise substantially from 5,000 to 200,000 Francs per aircraft. Secretly the RAeC may have hoped that this would deter entries and allow them to postpone the contest for a year.

To a large extent the RAeC had taken its eye off the ball by concentrating its efforts on the dispute with the FAI and French and Italian clubs, neglecting to try either to persuade its own government to fund a British team or to find an alternative. They had also ignored a very clear warning from the managers of Supermarine, Gloster and Napier, minuted back in October 1929, '… that their respective Companies would not wish to support another Contest unless the Regulations could be altered so as to lead to the production of a more useful type of machine'. They, too, believed the research programme for racers had run its course.

As a consequence of all the uncertainty and misdirected effort a crisis developed at the end of 1930 when the RAeC received entry fees for three aircraft each from Italy and France, yet they had no plans and had raised no funds with which to host the event. Furthermore the SBAC, which effectively meant Supermarine and Rolls-Royce, had stated bluntly that they would produce neither aircraft nor engines without receiving the same level of financial and technical support as for the previous contests. Both challenger nations were fully aware of the RAeC's predicament as it had been covered extensively in the press and parliament throughout the year.

Struggling with rising unemployment and the dire financial state of the nation the government remained focussed on social policies, holding firm to their decision throughout January 1931 despite repeated deputations from the RAeC and SBAC and negative reporting in parts of the popular press. In desperation the RAeC finally managed to extract grudging agreement that they would support the contest should the RAeC manage to raise the sum of £100,000 through public subscription by 4 February, which gave them only six days. A seemingly impossible task.

In the closing days of January, following a personal approach by the RAeC Chairman Sir Phillip Sassoon and a follow-up visit by Secretary Harold Perrin, the multimillionaire Lady Houston came forward with the whole sum, which was then passed on to the Air Ministry by the RAeC. It came with no contract, terms or conditions and the Ministry kept no accounts. Attempts initiated by Fred Handley-

LADY HOUSTON – THE MYTH SURROUNDING A GENEROUS WOMAN

It is well known that Lady Houston broke the impasse between the RAeC, SBAC and the government by underwriting the entire cost of the aircraft and engines for the British team and the organisation of the 1931 contest, but the circumstances that led up to this, the timing and reasons for her decision, and the consequences have been consistently misrepresented.

Lady Houston, born Fanny Lucy Radmall in 1857, was once divorced and twice widowed; three times if you include the ten years she spent living as the 'wife' of a brewery heir. The fortune she had accumulated from the settlements and wills of these men, Frederick Gretton, Theodore Brinckman, Baron Byron of Rochdale and finally Sir Robert Houston, had made her the richest woman in Britain.

She moved in high society circles through the late Victorian and Edwardian eras and grew to see herself as a woman of consequence, whose views should be heard and acted upon. She believed she had a winning personality and great beauty, and that men of wealth and power would naturally be attracted to her. While this may have had some substance in her youth, as she aged she harangued rather than influenced and maintained the illusion of youthful beauty through the increasingly liberal use of the re-toucher's brush in her published studio photographs.

Her political views shifted over the years as wealth and privilege moved her progressively out of touch with the issues affecting the bulk of the population, until in the post-First World War years she latched on to an increasingly fantasised view of the place of Britain in the world. This was a distorted, genteel, paternalistic version of the British Empire from the turn of the century, of conservative social order with elite leadership, and of the natural superiority of all things British. She reviled socialism in all its forms and those who promoted its merits, with particular venom reserved for Ramsay MacDonald, the leader of the Labour Party, who she was convinced was a closet Bolshevik determined to bring down the British establishment. Like many holding similar views she regarded herself as a bastion of patriotism, occupying the moral high ground and belittling those who held counter opinions. Despite this deep self-belief she most certainly neither knew more than, nor had superior foresight to, the many with whom she chose to do battle. Before 1931 she had shown scant interest in aviation.

Lady Houston visited Calshot to meet the British team preparing for the contest – one for which she had paid.

When Ramsay MacDonald announced that there was to be no government funding for a defence of the trophy, there is nothing to indicate that Lady Houston was either aware of this or interested. It was in the very last days of January 1931 when suddenly, and it would appear completely unexpectedly, she came forward with the money to enable the contest to be run. Had she suddenly, at the age of 73, developed a great passion for aviation or did she see this, perhaps, as a wonderful opportunity to humiliate the loathed MacDonald in public? The answer probably lies in her message to MacDonald and copied to the press: 'To prevent the socialist government from being spoilsports, Lady Houston will be responsible for all extra expenses beyond what Sir Philip Sassoon, president of the Royal Aero Club, says can be found, so that Great Britain can take part in the race for the Schneider trophy.' MacDonald did not respond, which irritated Lady Houston, as may well have been his intent.

In the aftermath of the Battle of Britain the story began to be told of how Lady Houston's funding of the 1931 contest had been crucial for the timely design and production of the Supermarine Spitfire and its Rolls-Royce Merlin engine, without which neither would have been ready in time for the war. This narrative was embellished in *The First of the Few*, a film released in 1942 as a semi-fictionalised story of the design of the Spitfire, produced with government blessing for propaganda purposes. Needless to say it played fast and loose with the reality: Britain then, and in the early post-war years, was all too willing to buy into the myth of mavericks, men and women with foresight, lone boffins and driven heroes battling a blinkered government bureaucracy and military inertia. However, stirring descriptions of Lady Houston as 'One of the Few' or 'Mother of the Spitfire' are in no way supported by the documented facts; at best it is gross exaggeration. The eleventh-hour work funded by her added little to the government-funded research in 1928–29 and was almost entirely irrelevant to the genesis of either the Spitfire or Merlin. Her funding for the 1931 contest, regardless of her underlying political agenda, was simply a fine sporting gesture that secured the trophy for Britain in perpetuity, and nothing more.

Lady Houston died on 29 December 1936 at the age of 79, just days after the abdication of King Edward VIII, an event that distressed her deeply.

RIGHT The official programme for the 1931 contest, at half the price of the 1929 edition – a clear sign of the financial state of the nation during the Depression.

BELOW Two of the architects of Britain's success in the Schneider Trophy contests: Sqn Ldr Augustus Orlebar, commanding officer of the HSF from 1929 to 1931, and Reginald Mitchell, Chief Engineer and Designer at Supermarine.

Page to have a RAeC committee oversee the expenditure were rebuffed. In the scant seven months that remained Lady Houston's money paid for the Admiralty to put in place boats and men to police the contest course, for the RAF to provide hangarage at Calshot, and for engines and aircraft to be constructed for the British team.

Supermarine and Rolls-Royce, of course, had been deeply involved in the discussions that took place prior to the government's about-face. Both had agreed that, should funding be approved by the end of January, there was just sufficient time to provide new engines and aircraft by modification of the 1929 types, although this was a policy which had proven unsuccessful for the USA in 1926 and Italy in 1927.

A succession of indifferent prototypes, a resultant lack of orders and the depressed state of the aircraft industry in general had left Supermarine with plenty of spare capacity in their works and, despite having to lay off a portion of the workforce, sufficient staff to undertake the construction work as a priority. Their reservations regarding the impractical nature of Schneider racers had been quietly laid aside. The two S6s were returned from the MAEE to undergo a thorough overhaul and jigs were built ready to construct two new fuselages and sets of wings and floats. True to their word Supermarine, and more significantly Rolls-Royce, did a remarkable job to achieve a substantial increase in speed above that of the S6 in the limited time available.

The HSF were engaged in training with the two S5s and the Gloster IVA while they awaited the arrival of the refurbished and new racers. Preparations started badly when the modified S6A, N247, suffered severe fuselage damage as a result of rudder and tailplane flutter and a few weeks later its sister aircraft, N248, sank after hitting a ship's wake on landing. Then the first flight attempts with the new S6B had to be aborted as a consequence of unexpected problems with the propeller and a wing had to be replaced after striking a barge. Eventually, training and development settled down, only to be brought to a shocking halt when Lt Jerry Brinton suffered a fatal crash on take-off in the rebuilt N247. The team regrouped and

LEFT Lt Jerry Brinton RN prepares for a training flight in the venerable S5, N219. He lost his life shortly after in a crash on take-off in S6A, N247.

BELOW The S6A, N248, sank after a landing accident but was recovered, stripped down, repaired and was back in service before the contest.

ABOVE Eight weeks before the contest the first Supermarine Rolls-Royce S6B is manoeuvred down the slipway at Supermarine's works in Woolston.

preparations were well in hand as the date of the contest approached. In France and Italy, however, preparations were in complete disarray.

France had failed to have any aircraft ready for the 1929 contest. Research and development had continued through 1930, primarily on new aircraft and engines as the 1929 racers, when they flew, were clearly inferior to the S6 and hence unlikely to be competitive in 1931. Disappointment with the

power and reliability of their Hispano-Suiza engines resulted in contracts being awarded to Lorraine and Renault for advanced new supercharged designs, but they both ran into serious design and development problems, thus leaving the completed racing aircraft from Bernard, Nieuport and Dewoitine standing idle without engines. The authorities were considering sending a team of uprated 1929 racers in their place, but that idea came to a

RIGHT Dewoitine's HD410 was built in time for the contest, but its Lorraine Radium inverted V12 engine was nowhere near ready. The racers from Bernard and Nieuport were left in the same situation.

shattering halt when pilot Bougault suffered a fatal crash in the Bernard HV120. The French team felt that they had no option other than to default in the summer. Questions in the French parliament later revealed that the Ministre de l'Air had spent 57 million francs (£457,000) on the programme since it was initiated in 1928, considerably more than Britain had spent over the same period.

Italy started 1930 with the Macchi M67 and Savoia-Marchetti S65 vying for an opportunity to take the world air speed record back from Supermarine. The choice fell on the S65, which was believed to be capable of exceeding the S6's speed by a greater margin. Preparations were well in hand when Dal Molin lost control of the aircraft on take-off and was killed when it plunged into the water. This was the second fatality that the RAV had suffered within six months.

For 1931 they decided to revert to their earlier policy of concentrating on a single engine and airframe combination, as the effort for 1929, covering four new aircraft and

engines, had proven costly and unsuccessful. Macchi started work on the Macchi-Castoldi MC72 while Fiat committed to build the AS6, a radical new engine based on the compact AS5 they had developed for their diminutive C29 racer. Two modified versions of the AS5 would be bolted together nose-to-nose to drive geared coaxial propeller shafts and contra-rotating propellers. There was no mechanical connection between the two engines but a single supercharger driven by the rear engine provided boost to both. It was a reasonably simple concept in theory but would prove to be fiendishly difficult to achieve.

The AS6 was run on the bench in the second half of 1930 and immediately suffered from a catalogue of destructive failures of the supercharger, induction system, ignition, connecting rods, valves and others that continued for months. Under pressure from above, Fiat managed to supply an engine rated at 2,400hp for installation in the MC72 in May 1931, but it was still far from reliable and prone

LEFT Despite well over a year of development the Fiat AS6 engine in the Macchi-Castoldi MC72 was dangerously unreliable. It would be two more years before the problems were resolved.

RIGHT The first S6B
on display for the
press and guests
at Calshot. Mitchell
is standing, deep in
thought, at the far
right.

BELOW The pilots
of the HSF pose for
the press in front of
the three remaining
S6 series racers at
Calshot.

to violent backfires. Ground and air tests failed
to resolve the issues and while demonstrating
the problem to Fiat engineers, Lt Giovanni Monti
made a high-speed, low-level pass in front
of them only to plunge into the water and die
instantly. Frantic attempts were made to rectify
the problem but by mid-August it was obvious
they could not do so in time. When a request
for a six-month postponement of the contest

was rejected, the Italian team also defaulted.
A directive was issued that on the day of the
contest the MC72 would make an attempt on
the absolute air speed record as the aircraft
was believed to be faster, potentially, than the
S6B that was also to make an attempt that
day. Lt Stanislao Bellini was selected for the
flight but on his first run down the speed course
a violent backfire ruptured the supercharger

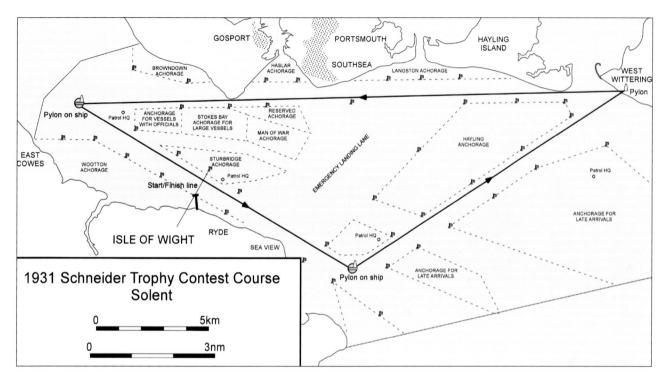

**1931 Schneider Trophy Contest Course
Solent**

0   5km

0   3nm

casing causing a ferocious fire. He flew into the surrounding hills and was killed instantly. After a further two years of development the aircraft was able to set a new absolute air speed record of 682.08km/hr (424mph), and a year later raised this to 709.2km/hr (440mph), both in the hands of Warrant Officer Francesco Agello. The record stood for five years.

This had been the worst preparatory period in the history of the contest and reinforced the view of many that the risks now far outweighed any rewards, and it was high time '... to put an end to this pernicious form of international rivalry' as it had been described by Philip Snowden, the Chancellor of the Exchequer. With no challengers for the trophy the contest was now destined to be a low-key and generally subdued affair, in stark contrast to 1929 when the flamboyant Italians had been present with their blood-red aircraft and numerous naval vessels. The Depression kept expenditure to a minimum so the festive atmosphere of the previous contest was generally lacking in the coastal towns adjacent to the course and the flotillas of yachts and pleasure craft that

had crowded the Solent were much reduced in number. The press days at Calshot prior to the contest were distinctly lacklustre with few interesting photo opportunities, because there was essentially nothing new to see. A revised contest course had been agreed for 1931, reducing the turns to three and placing one of the turn pylons onshore. Practice flying continued in the last few days.

ABOVE The contest course for 1931 had been modified to reduce the number of turns to three, with one of them located onshore.

RIGHT The onshore turn pylon near Henry Royce's home at West Wittering. The pylons were painted in a high visibility greenish yellow.

The day scheduled for the contest was a washout, heavy rain preventing any flying and forcing a one-day postponement. Many of the spectators who had made a daytrip to see the contest therefore missed out. Thankfully, the following day was clear, guests gathered at Calshot and the team prepared for the flights.

The Air Ministry made it clear that they were not prepared to sanction more than the bare minimum to secure the trophy, so should the first aircraft complete the course successfully there would be no further flights. In addition, this first run would be made at a comparatively low speed to maximise the chance of success.

So Flt Lt John Boothman took the S6B, S1595, around the course taking the turns by a wide margin and keeping the coolant water temperature at 95°C. Nevertheless his average speed for the course was 340mph, comfortably faster than the S6 in 1929. The trophy had been won.

ABOVE LEFT Sir Henry Royce in conversation with Sqn Ldr Orlebar.

ABOVE Reginald Mitchell accompanied by his wife talks with the RAeC Chairman Sir Phillip Sassoon.

BELOW Silhouetted against the glare of the sky the three British aircraft await the start of the contest.

ABOVE Boothman's S6B is brought ashore after his contest-winning flight.

RIGHT Boothman, with his mother and wife, meets the press after winning the trophy.

ABOVE Stainforth accelerates away in S1596 engulfed in spray. *(Jonathan Falconer)*

RIGHT The S6B, S1595, sets out for a pre-speed record test flight.

With the trophy secured the other two racers were stood down and S6B, S1596, was prepared for an attempt on the world air speed record. Flt Lt George Stainforth achieved 379.05mph, but it was known that the S6B was capable of more. Pressure on the Air Ministry led to them agreeing to allow one further attempt to be made before the HSF was disbanded. These plans were nearly thwarted when Stainforth capsized S1596 on landing after a test flight, caused by the heel of his shoe jamming under the rudder pedal. Fortuitously the aircraft did not have the special 'sprint' engine installed at the time so this was available for S1595. On 9 September Stainforth set out to make a final attempt to raise the speed record further. With his accumulated experience from the speed runs in the Gloster Napier VI in 1929 and the first record in the S6B, he had ascertained the optimal technique to fly over the speed course and was able to push the S6B to a new record of 407.5mph. The 28mph increase over the previous record was attributed to an increase in engine power (39%), reduction in drag (10%), increase in propeller efficiency (14%) and improvement in piloting (37%).

RIGHT The heroes of the day, George Stainforth and John Boothman.

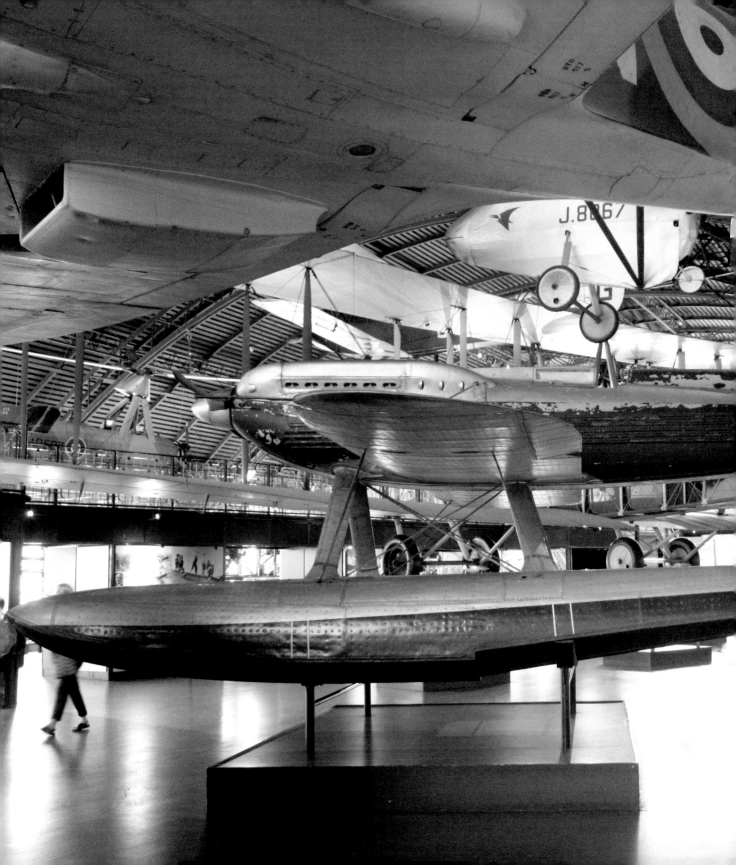

Chapter Eight

Supermarine Schneider Trophy survivors

The ultimate fate of most Supermarine racers was at the hands of the scrap yards. However, two aircraft avoided the cutter's blowtorch and have interesting stories to tell.

OPPOSITE The Supermarine Rolls-Royce S6B in the Science Museum lurks in the gloom, tucked away beneath the wings of other exhibits. A good camera and a steady hand are essential to photographers.

Two of the four S6 series airframes have survived – S6A, N248, and S6B, S1595. The second S6A, N247, was destroyed in Lt Brinton's fatal crash in 1931; and the second S6B, S1596, which sank after a landing accident, was recovered with minor damage but not repaired. Lady Houston laid claim to both S6Bs but this was denied by the government.

N248 had flown in the 1929 contest and was the third aircraft in the team for 1931, refurbished after bouncing and sinking following a hurried landing after a practice flight. In 1932 it was offered to Southampton Borough Council but was not accepted by them until 1937; in the interim it was presumably in storage with Supermarine. The aircraft was loaned to Leslie Howard and his film production company in 1942 for use in *The First of the Few*, for which the engine bay was mocked up to represent the S5 that won the Schneider Trophy at Venice in 1927, but with registration N247 and racing number '2' applied for the 1929 winner. After the war, paint supplier Cellon repainted the aircraft for exhibition at the 1946

Southampton air display and marked it 'S6B' on the tail. It was subsequently placed on display at Southampton Airport, Eastleigh. In 1951 it formed part of the aviation display in the Transport Pavilion at the Festival of Britain, now carrying the erroneous markings of S6B, S1596, and with race number '7', following which it was placed back in storage in a hangar at Eastleigh. In 1957 it was exhibited on the observation roof terrace of the newly opened Queen's Building at Heathrow Airport and the next year taken from storage and placed on permanent display on the Royal Pier at Southampton. On at least two occasions, in 1959 and 1968, it was included in a line-up of RAF aircraft on Horse Guards Parade in London.

The error in the identification of the aircraft was finally realised in the 1970s and a new home was procured for it in a converted scout hut in the centre of Southampton, refitted to house the new R.J. Mitchell Museum. Prior to display a full restoration and repaint, as N248, was carried out by the British Hovercraft Corporation at Cowes. In the 1980s N248 was

BELOW The Supermarine Rolls-Royce S6A, N248, is one of many excellent aviation exhibits in the Solent Sky Museum, Southampton.

moved to the new-build Solent Sky Museum close to the Itchen waterfront and nearly opposite the site of Supermarine's Woolston works where it had been built. A more recent repaint, including a lurid green interior, has improved the weatherproofing and the aircraft has been taken out of the museum for display on several occasions, including visits to the RAF Museum in Hendon, and to Calshot and Goodwood. On the occasion of the centenary of the partnership of Rolls and Royce, N248 was suspended from a pylon at Goodwood House alongside Sir Malcolm Campbell's *Bluebird* car and speed boat. Although this was less than dignified treatment for a rare aircraft it did at least demonstrate the robustness of Mitchell's design.

S6B, S1595, was placed on display at Vickers' London showrooms shortly after the 1931 contest and speed record and was then transferred to the Motor Exhibition at Olympia where it was exhibited suspended from the ceiling. In November 1931 the aircraft was on display in the Science Museum in South Kensington and was presented to them in

1932, where it has remained on display for most of the time since. It has been moved on several occasions as the museum expanded and reorganised its galleries and has been in the Flight Gallery since 1961. At the time of writing the gallery is desperately overcrowded.

The museum's policy is one of conservation and to minimise restoration, although their records indicate that many of the aircraft on display, especially those with fabric covering, had actually been recovered and repainted on or before delivery and some have been so treated again over the years. The records for the S6B are incomplete. The dark blue paint does not appear to be appropriate for the colours adopted by Supermarine for their racing aircraft, and on the floats this is seen to overlay an early brighter blue that is more likely to be the original paintwork. It may well have been partly repainted prior to delivery to the museum as the unburnt fuel and exhaust during the speed record runs acted as a highly efficient paint stripper. To reduce the possibility of damage to the exhibits from light, the gallery had its ceiling repainted from

ABOVE The S6A has made several trips away from its home at Solent Sky. Here it is on display at Goodwood airfield.

RIGHT The S6A was hung from a pylon sculpture outside Goodwood House alongside Sir Malcolm Campbell's *Bluebird* speed record car and boat as part of the Rolls-Royce centenary celebrations in 2004.

cream to dark blue many years ago and the side windows were obscured progressively by blinds and cabinets. Electric lighting is minimal. Yet the years have not been kind to the S6B, especially over recent decades, and it is a matter of concern to the conservation specialists. There has been significant peeling and loss of the dark blue paint on the fuselage and degradation of the fabric on the rudder. The floats, however, despite years of people touching them, appear largely unaffected. The

open cockpit has accumulated a significant covering of dust.

Two of the Rolls-Royce 'R' engines that were flown in the S6Bs have survived. Engine R27, the sprint engine that was installed in S1595 for the speed record and subsequently in George Eyston's land speed record car *Thunderbolt*, is in the Flight Gallery in the Science Museum. R25, which flew in the second S6B, S1596, and was also used in *Thunderbolt*, is now on display in the RAF Museum, Hendon.

BELOW The loss of blue paint from the S6B, S1595, since the 1970s is very noticeable.

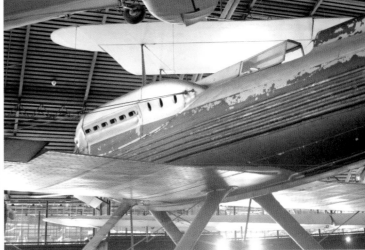

Sources

Aeronautical Research Committee, *1927 Schneider Trophy Contest – Collected Reports on British High Speed Aircraft*, Reports and Memoranda No 1300 (London, HMSO, 1931)

Aeronautical Research Committee, *Collected Reports on British High Speed Aircraft for the 1931 Schneider Trophy Contest*, Reports and Memoranda No 1575 (London, HMSO, 1934)

Aeronautical Research Committee, *Tests on Quarter-scale Models of High-speed Seaplanes for the Schneider Trophy Contest, 1929*, Report T.3000 1930 (The National Archives, DSIR 23/3014)

Air Ministry, *Notes on High Speed Flight 1931 – collected by Wing Commander A.H. Orlebar*, Report T.3209 1932 (The National Archives, AVIA 13/112)

Banks, F.R., 'The Evolution of the Schneider Engine', *The Aeroplane,* Vol XLI ,No 15, 7 October 1931, pp. 864–72

Banks, Air Cdre F.R., 'Memories of the Last Schneider Trophy Contests', *Centenary Journal – Royal Aeronautical Society,* Vol 70, No 661, January 1966, pp. 179–80

Banks, Air Cdre F.R., *I Kept No Diary* (London, Airlife Publications, 1978)

Biard, Capt H.C., *Wings* (London, Hurst & Blackett Ltd, 1934)

Buchanan, Maj J.S., 'The Schneider Cup Race, 1925', *Journal of the Royal Aeronautical Society*, January 1926

D'Arcy Greig, Air Cdre D., *My Golden Flying Years* (London, Grubb Street, 2010)

Flight, 'Winner of the Schneider Race', *Flight*, 16 February 1928, pp. 94–99

Flight, 'The Napier Lion Racing Engine', *Flight,* 26 April 1928, pp. 280–84

Hollis Williams, D.L., 'The Racing Airscrews of 1931', *The Aircraft Engineer Supplement to Flight,* Vol XXIII, No 44, 30 October 1931, pp. 1086a–c

Holroyd, F., 'Racing Seaplanes', *Journal of the Royal Aeronautical Society*, February 1930, pp. 423–35

J.T., 'How the Supermarine S.6B was built', *The Aeroplane,* Vol XLI No 25, 16 December 1931, pp. 1376–79

Mitchell, R.J., 'Tank Tests with Seaplane Models', *Aircraft Engineering*, October 1930, pp. 255–259

Mitchell, R.J., 'Racing Seaplanes and their influence on Design', *Aeronautical Engineering Supplement to Aeroplane*, Vol XXXVII, No 26, 25 December 1929, pp. 1429–30

Mitchell, R.J., 'Schneider Trophy Machine Design, 1927', *Journal of the Royal Aeronautical Society*, Proceedings, third meeting, second half, 63rd Session 1928, pp. 744–62

Orlebar, Wg Cdr A.H., *Schneider Trophy* (London, Seeley Service & Co, 1932)

Pegram, Ralph, *Schneider Trophy Racing Seaplanes and Flying Boats* (Fonthill, 2012)

Ralli, P., 'Design of Airscrews for Schneider Trophy Race 1927', *Journal of the Royal Aeronautical Society*, Proceedings, third meeting, second half, 63rd Session 1928, pp. 763–67

Rolls-Royce, 'The Rolls-Royce racing engines', *Flight,* Vol XXIII, No 40, 2 October 1931, pp. 989–95

Schofield, H.M, *The High Speed and Other Flights* (London, John Hamilton Ltd, 1932)

Snaith, Grp Capt Leonard, 'Memories of the 1931 Schneider Trophy Contest', in *R.J. Mitchell, Schooldays to Spitfire* (London, 3rd edition, Tempus Publishing, 2002)

Stainforth, Flt Lt G.H., 'British methods of high speed flying and training of pilots', in *5th Volta Conference – Le Alte Velocita in Aviazione* (Rome, Reale Accademia D'Italia, 1936)

Waghorn, Flt Lt H.R.W, 'The Schneider Trophy, 1929', *Journal of the Royal Aeronautical Society*, May 1930, pp. 400–08

Supermarine Rolls-Royce S6B specification

Aircraft		
Length	Overall	28ft 10in
	Fuselage	25ft 3in
	Floats	24ft 0in
Track of floats		7ft 6in
Beam of floats		2ft 8in
Depth of floats		2ft 8in
Reserve buoyancy	Port	80%
	Starboard	39%
Span	Main plane	30ft 0in
Chord	Main plane	5ft 8in
Span	Tailplane	8ft 1.5in
Height		12ft 3in
Weight	Fully loaded for contest	6,086lb
	Empty	4,590lb
Area	Main plane	145sq ft
Aerofoil section	Main plane	RAF27
Wing loading		44lb/sq ft
Area	Fixed tailplane	15.8sq ft
	Elevator	6.0sq ft
	Fin	6.0sq ft
	Rudder	7.5sq ft
	Wing radiators	235sq ft
	Float radiators	145sq ft
	Oil cooling	67.8sq ft
Fuel tank capacity	Port	48gal
	Starboard	110gal
Water		25.36gal
Oil		23.25gal

Engine		
Rolls-Royce 'R'		Water-cooled V12
Bore		6in
Stroke		6.6in
Volume		36.7 litres
Weight		1,640lb
Compression ratio		6:1
Boost	For contest	18lb/sq in
Max permissible RPM	For contest	3,200
Idle RPM		475 (200 minimum)
Gear ratio		0.605
Full throttle power	Contest	2,330hp
	Speed record	2,500hp
BMEP	At normal RPM	254lb/sq in
Fuel consumption	At normal RPM	0.6pt/BHP/hr
	Speed record	0.85pt/BHP/hr
Oil consumption	Approx.	14gal/hr
Spark plugs		Lodge X170
Magnetos		BTH or Watford

Performance		
Maximum level speed	Contest configuration	372mph
	Speed record configuration	390mph
Speed record, 3km course	Contest configuration	379.05mph
	Speed record configuration	407.50mph

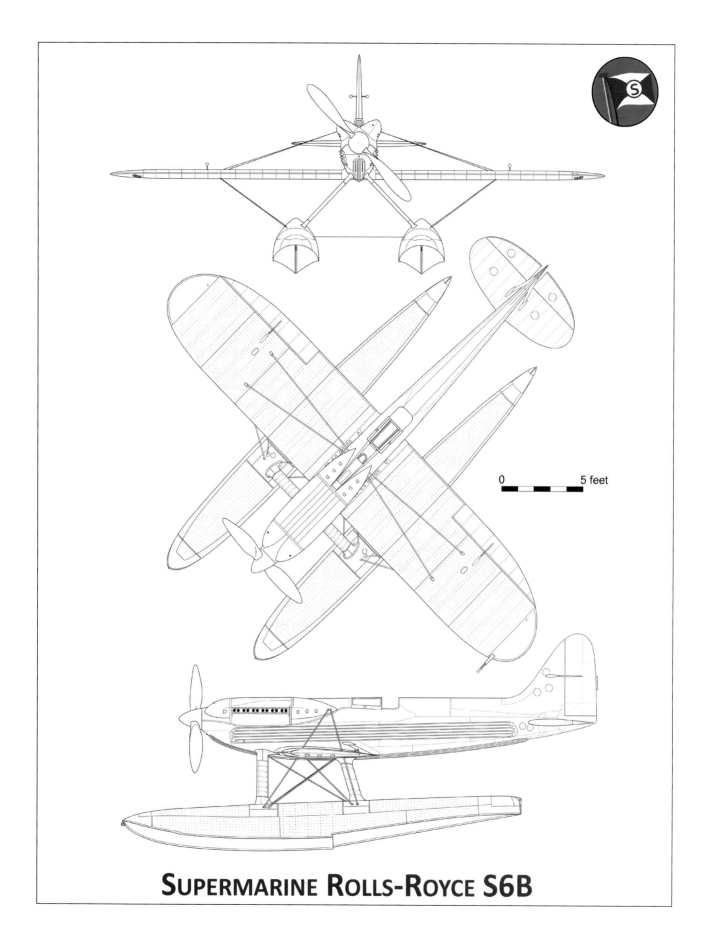

0 ▬▬▬▬▬ 5 feet

SUPERMARINE ROLLS-ROYCE S6B

Index